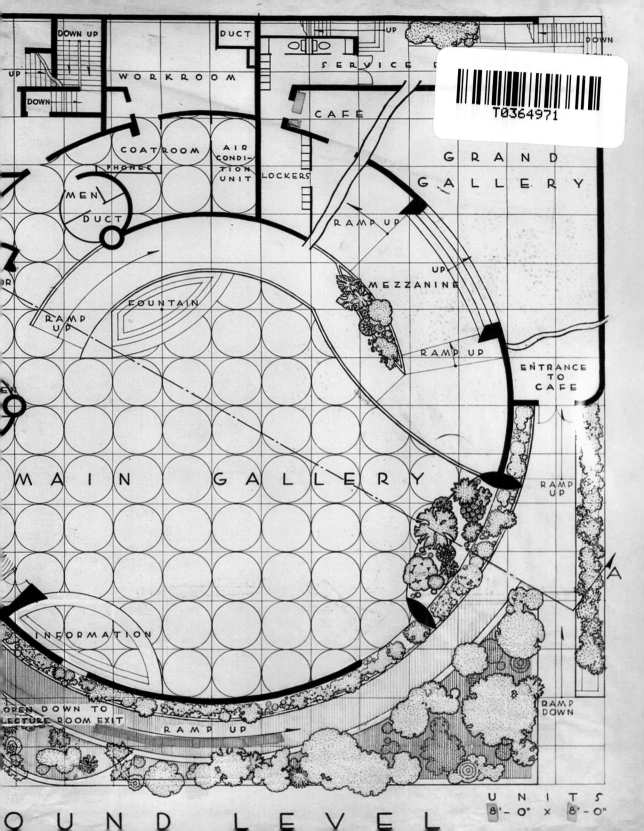

WORKROOM

DUCT

SERVICE

CAFE

COATROOM

AIR
CONDI-
TION
UNIT

PHONES

LOCKERS

GRAND
GALLERY

DOWN UP

UP

DOWN

UP

DOWN

DOWN

MEN

DUCT

RAMP UP

UP

MEZZANINE

FOUNTAIN

RAMP
UP

RAMP UP

ENTRANCE
TO
CAFE

RAMP
UP

MAIN GALLERY

A

INFORMATION

RAMP
DOWN

OPEN DOWN TO
LECTURE ROOM EXIT

RAMP UP

OUND LEVEL

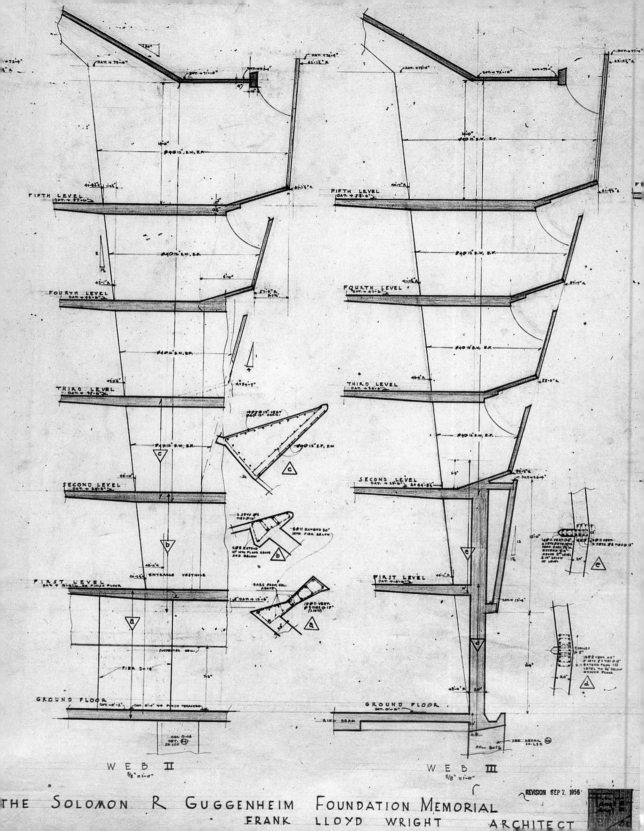

THE SOLOMON R GUGGENHEIM FOUNDATION MEMORIAL
FRANK LLOYD WRIGHT ARCHITECT

The
Guggenheim

The Guggenheim

Frank Lloyd Wright's Iconoclastic Masterpiece

Francesco Dal Co

Translated by Sarah Melker

Great Architects/Great Buildings

Yale University Press
New Haven and London

yalebooks.com/art

The translation of this work has been funded by SEPS
Segretariato Europeo per le Pubblicazioni Scientifiche

Via Val d'Aposa 7 - 40123 Bologna - Italy
seps@seps.it - www.seps.it

The present volume is a completely revised version of the book
Il tempo e l'architetto, published in 2004 by Mondadori Electa,
Milan.

Typeset by Tina Henderson based on a design by Luke Bulman
Set in Atlas Grotesk
Printed in China through Oceanic Graphic International, Inc.

Library of Congress Control Number: 2016960143
ISBN 978-0-300-22605-8
A catalogue record for this book is available from
the British Library.

This paper meets the requirements of
ANSI/NISO Z39.48-1992 (Permanence of Paper).

10 9 8 7 6 5 4 3 2 1

Cover illustration: Guggenheim Museum. Interior view before
the 1959 opening
Endpapers: Guggenheim Museum. Drawings, main floor plan,
1953, and structural details of webs, 1956
Frontispiece: Guggenheim Museum. Perspective drawing, 1944
Epigraph, preface: Italo Calvino, *Hermit in Paris:
Autobiographical Writings*, trans. Jonathan Cape (New York:
Mariner Books, 2014), pp. 42–43.
Epigraph, chapter one: Richard Serra, *Writings/Interviews*
(Chicago: University of Chicago Press, 1994), pp. 104, 109.

Contents

Preface

*In the last few weeks the obligatory topic of every
New York conversation is the new museum designed by
Frank Lloyd Wright to house Solomon Guggenheim's
art collection. It has just been opened. Everyone
criticizes it; I am a fanatical supporter of it, but I find
myself nearly always on my own in this. The building
is a kind of spiral tower, a continuous ascending ramp
without steps, with a glass cupola. As you go up and
look out you always have a different view with perfect
proportions, since there is a semi-circular outcrop
that offsets the spiral, and down below there is a small
slice of elliptical flower-bed and a window with a tiny
glimpse of a garden, and these elements, changing
at whatever height you are now at, are an example of
architecture in movement of unique precision and
imagination. Everyone claims that the architecture
dominates the paintings and it is true (apparently
Wright hated painters), but what does it matter? You
go there primarily to see the architecture, and then
you see the paintings always well and uniformly
illuminated, which is the main thing.*
—Italo Calvino, 1959

The Solomon R. Guggenheim Museum, the subject of this
book, shows how even a contemporary building can be an
example of "timeless architecture" (my chosen translation
of *architettura di sempre*, a concept inspired by Max Weber
that I have often explored in my writings). I use this term to
distinguish a work that does not "throw itself into the abyss
as soon as its riddle has been solved," as the poet Heinrich
Heine wrote. Buildings of this kind—and their meanings—do
not belong to an epoch, a specific culture, or a geographical
area; no "ism" applies to them, and they possess a language
that is able to communicate universally. They are works that
are not bound by the same constraints, however necessary,
that historians face in studying them: construction, purpose,
client objectives, financial limitations, available materials,
the technical knowledge of the builders, or the project's

ambition—in short, everything that makes studying the intrinsically unstable architecture of the past "sweet poison," as Richard Krautheimer said.

Our own era, like every period of time, is subject to a continuous movement; it is transformed and in turn recasts the certainties from which it grew into enigmas, and facts into new question marks. This does not change with a narrower historical perspective or shorter time frame. On the contrary, a tighter focus often yields greater complexities, and the most difficult task for the historian is to trace them. The threads of the warp stretched on the loom, together with the weft that crisscrosses them, form the cloth that the historian must examine in order to interpret its nature, meaning, and identity. This task becomes more complicated still when the warp is not taut, and picking out the threads of the weft involves unraveling the knots that bind the strings in a tangle. The story that I recount here is not a neat skein. These threads ply across different planes and directions, with different lengths, layers, and knots that result not from the mechanical bustle of the loom's shuttle, but rather from the unpredictable movement of life.

Like mercury poured on a marble surface, the "story" of Frank Lloyd Wright's Guggenheim Museum breaks up into many disparate plots. Telling it was thus an exercise in patience, involving a continual shuttling between events, episodes, and circumstances that arose and resurfaced and that never truly concluded. In trying to impose an order on these events, without any confidence in their chronology, I have emphasized the important role that the passing of time played in the construction of the Guggenheim Museum. The seventeen years that separate the moment that Wright was commissioned to design the work and the day the museum was inaugurated reveal the innumerable difficulties that had to be overcome to build this unique work, which was itself conceived by men in the twilight of their lives. The many years it took are echoed in the many ways that time's influence can be seen in the building's extraordinary composition, which we still admire today. In other words, Walter Benjamin's "Angel of History," who turns his back on the future and fixes his gaze on the past, has no role in this history. Instead, time acted as Wright's constant companion throughout the creating of the Guggenheim; its "power to build" shaped the process itself. This is unusual, as time and its consequences generally set in after a work is completed, when its original meaning has long departed.

This unsought alliance between Wright and time, the "great builder," could not have been formed if the architect had not first provided—or rather, offered—his know-how, obstinacy, imagination, and cynicism. These qualities are shared in the makeup, and the inherent interrelationship, of the ideas driving the building's structure and static conception—contingent and effective proof of Wright's continuing exercise in "discretion," as a "quest of freedom in deciding." The most surprising point in the Guggenheim story is how discretion, in this sense, forms the base of the construction's materiality—that is, the ways in which the museum was conceived in engineering terms and then physically built. I considered these processes, among many less tenable, as among the most resilient threads in this metaphorical warp.

In addition to the role of time and the building's structure, the third major theme in this narrative concerns the very idea of a museum, a concept that was at the heart of Wright's project. Visiting the Guggenheim, going over its story, and reading Wright's words recalled the many times that contemporary culture has reacted against the "historical fetishism" that has led museums, which Hans Sedlmayr termed "pompous asylums for the homeless," to take the place in the modern city that cathedrals once held. "Today, if I go to the Louvre," wrote Alberto Giacometti, ". . . all those works have had such a miserable air—quite a miserable trajectory, so precarious, a stammering approximation over the course of centuries, in all possible directions yet extremely concise, primary, naïve, in order to delimit a formidable immensity, that I looked despairingly at the living." Giorgio Manganelli observed that in museums "each item is prey—bought, captured, deported, unearthed, excavated, stolen, corrupted, mistaken, smuggled. A museum presupposes a passion that is not oblivious to crimes, somber concentration, the mythological fantasy of being able to carve out a flat and bounded space, Ptolemaic in Copernicus' spherical world." While writing about the Guggenheim I had before my eyes similar images, and it is for this reason that I spoke of it as an iconoclastic museum, and not only because "you go there primarily to see the architecture," as Italo Calvino remarked in 1959. Rather, I tried to emphasize the heretical originality of a work representing the zenith of the career of a great architect whose guiding light was his aversion to the "authority of orthodoxy."

It is from this perspective, too, that I believe it appropriate to consider the Guggenheim as a metonym for Wright himself. But metonymy is not exhausted by a single meaning. Rather, as Yves Bonnefoy has written and I have attempted to express in these pages, it "plunges into the depths of the past, reopens the mind to the thought of chance, and thus to the irreversible passage of time, to the intuition of finiteness."

I don't think there is any possibility for architecture to be a work of art. I've always thought that art was nonfunctional and useless. Architecture serves needs which are specifically functional and useful. Therefore, architecture as a work of art is a contradiction in terms. . . .

When the architect's ego impinges and his design interferes with the nature of how art can be viewed, real problems result. I would think that architects would be both tolerant and supportive of the kind of invention that occurs in art and would come to understand that they are basically in a service profession, not an artistic endeavor.
—Richard Serra

Chapter One
The Guggenheim

Following a complicated confrontation between Frank Lloyd Wright, his consultants, and the Board of Standards and Appeals, the City of New York granted a construction permit for the new museum in March 1956, four years after the trustees of the Solomon R. Guggenheim Foundation had approved the plans. The project violated several regulations in the construction code of the time, and in all likelihood the permit would not have been approved without the energetic intercession of Robert Moses, a powerful figure who shaped the history of New York in the twentieth century and, as we will see, played a significant role in the matter at hand. A few months later, on August 16, ground was broken and construction of the Solomon R. Guggenheim Museum began. At the time, Frank Lloyd Wright was eighty-nine years old; he was born on June 8, 1867, in Richland Center, Wisconsin. In 1954, he had moved into a suite at the Plaza Hotel in New York in order to oversee the work commissioned by the Guggenheim Foundation for the building of the museum. He adapted the suite (previously occupied by the French couturier Christian Dior) to his needs, decorating the rooms with Asian art and lacquered furniture produced in his own studio, and he called it "Taliesin the Third" or "Taliesin East," a playful reference to his other studios—Taliesin in Spring Green, Wisconsin, and Taliesin West in Scottsdale, Arizona. He made the suite the marker of a further chapter appended to his enduring autobiographical, esthetic exaltation of life, which as Lewis Mumford put it "could be described, from first to last, as a 'Song of Myself.'"

When the Guggenheim Museum was opened to the public, on October 21, 1959, six months had passed since Wright's death on April 9. A few months after the permit was issued, on December 12, 1956, the *New York Times* published an open letter inviting Wright's clients to rethink the proposed project. It is likely that James Johnson Sweeney—at the time director of the Guggenheim—was among those who had a hand in writing the letter. Hilla Rebay, who had from the start been the Guggenheim Foundation's curator, disparagingly called Sweeney a "businessman"; and in an interview in 1966, one year prior to her death, she did not hesitate to confess that she "always thought he was an impostor." But these judgments are only useful in that they allow a glimpse of the complicated and tense relations between the protagonists of the present story; we will also look at Sweeney's role in the Guggenheim Museum from 1952—when the building plans were on the verge of being approved—to 1960. For now, let us note that after leaving the Guggenheim Museum Sweeney moved to Houston to serve as director of the Museum of Fine Arts there. The Houston museum had recently been expanded, between 1954 and 1958, thanks to the bequest of Nina J. Cullinan in 1953. The building extension was designed by Ludwig Mies van der Rohe, whom Sweeney would later commission for the construction of the Brown Pavilion, begun in 1961. While Sweeney's choices after 1960 allow us to imagine what he might have thought of the museum Wright began to build in 1956 for the Guggenheim Foundation, the fact remains that among the twenty-one signatories to the letter published by the *New York Times* were artists such as Willem de Kooning, Adolph Gottlieb, Franz Kline, and Robert Motherwell. They were members of an intellectual circle to which Wright did not belong, and their artistic experiences were far from those of Hilla Rebay's youth and to which she devoted herself throughout her life. The immediate goal of the petitioners was to induce the Guggenheim Foundation to abandon the idea, fervently defended by Wright, of displaying the collection's works under natural light, laid along the inclined walls planned for the museum—a continuous surface that the architect described as "a curving wave that never breaks." The appeal, published a few months after construction had started and that Sweeney obviously could not sign, made plain the causes of symptoms that had been perceptible for some time. Its effects marked the history of the museum and influenced many who took on the challenge of interpreting Wright's work.

Like the writers of the letter to the *New York Times*, a number of artists, critics, architects, and historians followed a conventional perspective in identifying the museum as the ground for a bitter clash between art and architecture. Wright himself had predicted such a confrontation. Brewing trouble can be seen as early as August 1943 in a letter from Wright to

Rebay, only a few months after Guggenheim had commissioned him to design the museum. As though wishing to pre-emptively dispel this danger, and at the same time convince Rebay, who had brought Wright onto the project, Wright sent her a message. In it he emphasized certain key phrases by placing them in parentheses, and for the rest paraphrased nineteenth-century scholar of Japanese studies Ernest F. Fenollosa: "Architecture (there is none in New York City) is the mother-art of arts. Where she really is she is not likely to murder her infants or frustrate her sons and daughters. The trouble is sometimes her upstarts do not know their own mother—the brats."

Yet it was the grueling process of design and construction that shaped the museum. Seventeen years passed between the first sketches and the museum's inauguration. The Guggenheim Museum clearly demonstrates how many of the greatest buildings in the history of architecture have resulted from the harmonization of the architect's work with the passing of time. By 1959 those walking along Fifth Avenue in New York could see the Guggenheim Museum, which possessed an "indescribable individuality," as Mumford admitted without changing his "sadly unfavorable" opinion of the building. With its modest dimensions and extraordinary form—like a shard, streamlined by the median band above the entrance enveloping and structuring the ascending volumes, irregularly shaped, seemingly jointless, rooted in the Manhattan soil—the museum's spiral rises away from the ground, "flowing and growing," like the forms depicted in "the book of nature written in the language of geometry," as Galileo wrote. For this reason it also evokes illustrations from the drawing manual *Ryakuga Haya-oshie* by Katsushika Hokusai (1812), one of the Japanese artists Wright admired from an early age. Indeed, Wright attributed to Hokusai certain gifts he felt they shared, the foundations of all "grammar and syntax," as Wright wrote in 1912 in his *The Japanese Print: An Interpretation*. He believed Hokusai recognized "the first elements constituting the skeleton of the structure," which are translated "in a stringent simplification by elimination of the insignificant." And the passing of time is no stranger to the accomplishment of this end.

The museum sits on a lot bounded by Fifth Avenue, 88th Street, and 89th Street, overlooking Central Park. The upturned spiral Wright built there still bears marks of the adversity it had to overcome, seizing from Manhattan the scrap of land that it occupies. Fused into its symbolism, Wright

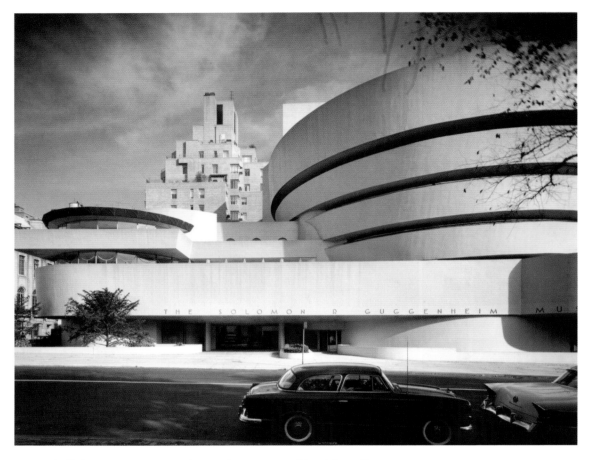

poured all that he had learned over the course of his life, influenced by Victor Hugo's *Hunchback of Notre-Dame*, books by Kakuzo Okakura, as well as memories from Fenollosa's lectures (and clearly, from Japanese prints, those "intoxicating things" he had been introduced to by the cousin of Joseph Silsbee, his first employer). The building takes possession of the site, claiming the right to the disconnectedness it enjoys, challenging with its sealed finiteness the endless uniformity, random incompleteness, and banality of its host city.

It is in this sense alone that the Guggenheim might be associated with images or ideas stemming from a scene of conflict. It is possible to make this connection, provided that one carefully distinguishes the figures of the contenders and, above all, considers the construction as an essential representation of a labyrinth, or rather of an epiphany. Paradoxically, the

The Solomon R. Guggenheim Museum seen from Fifth Avenue

The main interior space of the Guggenheim Museum before the opening, 1959

Guggenheim is precisely what a building housing a museum—a shelter for the relics of the shipwrecks of history—should not be, as is usually thought. Its shell and its convexity contrast its order and form with any other object that casually towers over an expanse of a few blocks of New York. The upturned spiral of the construction Wright designed exposes and illuminates an endless disruption. It spins from an artificial plane that appears to support the whole structure; it wrests away from the Babel surrounding it that patch of earth from which it rises—making an overturned Tower of Babel a powerful metaphor, a theater of the city transformed into a world stage for Wright's final act in life.

Thus it does not belong among the myriad examples of the conflict between art and architecture. The story of the Guggenheim Museum yields something unlike what those who commissioned it feared; it differs, too, from Mumford's judgment expressed in the *New Yorker* in December 1959: "But architecture is not simply sculpture, and this building was meant also to serve as a museum. In that context it is an audacious failure." The common thread that brought Mumford, and several others after him, to observe that "you may go to this building to see Kandinsky or Jackson Pollock; you remain to see Frank Lloyd Wright," is, not surprisingly, the greatest homage to Wright's work, and while it unintentionally illuminates the building's deepest meaning, it explains only one aspect of the story of the Guggenheim Museum. To this day it remains a compelling story, and one that is particularly instructive not only for those who share Mies van der Rohe's conviction that architecture's great merit is that it gives names to the epochs of civilization. The strands of this story make up a dense fabric of extraordinary, curious, banal, and unpredictable events, knotted up with misunderstandings, clashes, blandishments, confusion, and compromises, which Wright disentangled both laboriously and masterfully, allowing him to approach the end of his life while working on the building that crowned it. The Guggenheim Museum is the work that, more than any other, patently reveals the many distinct tensions that can be perceived and observed in Wright's life. It does so by evoking the phases in his unparalleled career and his majestic old age—"one of our giant redwoods has fallen," Mumford wrote in his obituary—and shows that they do not fit with the clichés so often used to interpret them.

Chapter Two

Solomon Guggenheim, Hilla Rebay, Their Art Collection, and MoMA

Skimming the main points alone is enough to show why the Guggenheim evokes an aloof detachment, even to the point of self-conceit. In retelling the story, it is important to remember that the building's present name, the "Guggenheim Museum," is only the latest in a series of different appellations. For his part, Solomon originally called it "Hilla's Museum." After 1949, however, in the crucial phases of Wright's relations with his clients, and in particular with Harry Guggenheim, his patron's nephew and heir, Wright referred to the building as the "Solomon R. Guggenheim Memorial." Having taken into account the building's continuous and thus expressive change of names—a subject we will return to—the individuals attached to them deserve our attention. Who were Solomon and Hilla? How did their fates intertwine, preparing the foundations upon which Wright would achieve his masterpiece?

Solomon R. Guggenheim (1861–1949) belonged to one of the wealthiest families in the United States; the Guggenheim fortune came from mining, and Solomon's wife, Irene (1868–1954), was a Rothschild. Solomon collected ancient art, while Irene was a socialite in the sophisticated New York world whose tastes were growing toward contemporary art. In 1927, through her sister and Gertrude Vanderbilt Whitney, the leading collector of American art, Irene met a German painter, Baroness Hildegard (Hilla) Rebay von Ehrenwiesen (1890–1967). Hilla had arrived in the United States only a few months earlier, probably invited by Marie Sterner, who had opened her first New York gallery in 1923. Among the letters of introduction Rebay carried with her when leaving Germany was one addressed to Solomon Guggenheim from Gertrude de Paats, Irene's sister. At the time the baroness was thirty-seven and already had a vibrant life behind her. She had cultivated friendships and met people in the artistic circles she had assiduously frequented from her early youth, where she had encountered some of the luminaries of the European avant-garde.

Rebay was descended from Alsatian nobility and had
studied in Paris at the Académie Julian, as well as in Munich,
and she felt at home in Italy. A friend of Félix Fénéon, the
Parisian critic and writer whose famous portrait by Paul Signac
can be admired at the Museum of Modern Art in New York,
Rebay met Hans Arp in Zurich in 1915 through the "mercurial"
composer Ferruccio Busoni. With Arp she had enjoyed a
passionate as well as earnestly intellectual relationship, which
reinforced her interest in *Gegenstandslos*, "non-objective,"
art, and in Wassily Kandinsky's work. Hilla had taken part in
the initiatives of the Zurich Dadaist group, the soirées organized at the Cabaret Voltaire by Hugo Ball and frequented by
Arp. In 1916, she began a relationship in Berlin with one of the
"founding fathers" of the twentieth-century avant-garde,
Herwarth Walden. Subsequently, she exhibited her paintings
in the Galerie Der Sturm, which Walden had opened in Berlin
to celebrate the publication of the hundredth issue of the
eponymous journal, which he had founded in 1910. Moving
across Europe from city to city, she became friends with,
among others, Kurt Schwitters, Hans Richter, Max Ernst, and
Piet Mondrian. In the circles linked to Der Sturm, she had met
Rudolf Bauer, a renowned illustrator, and at the time Walden's
assistant. Around 1921, after distancing himself from Der
Sturm, Bauer wanted to make himself the promoter of an

artistic movement—best to call it a combination of a gallery and a milieu—analogous to the one formed around Walden's Berlin gallery. Bauer decided to call it Das Geistreich, The Kingdom of Spirit, and this name was later given to the gallery he founded in 1930 thanks to support from Guggenheim, who in the meantime had begun to appreciate his paintings, having been introduced to them by Rebay. In 1938, Das Geistreich was closed down by the Nazi regime as a manifestation of "degenerate art"—*Entartete Kunst*, the name given to the 1937 exhibition in Munich of 650 works seized on Joseph Goebbels's orders from many German museums, and which Hilla had visited—and Bauer was jailed. The next year he moved to the United States, where Guggenheim offered him a contract, though one that guaranteed him only a somewhat paltry monthly stipend.

The encounter with Bauer, destined to mark the life of the still young painter, soon transformed into a tempestuous love affair, made difficult by his fractious personality and their straitened circumstances, with Rebay painting portraits on commission to make ends meet. Bauer was appreciated by collectors such as Katherine S. Dreier and was tormented by delusory ambitions. It was he who brought about the depressing end to their relationship in 1944, though he had found in Rebay an extraordinary and loyal supporter. Together, in Berlin, they had frequented the avant-garde circles and the November Group and brought to life their own group, Der Krater; they shared a studio next to Erich Mendelsohn's, with whom they were on friendly terms. It is not surprising that when some twenty years later Rebay was thinking about which architect to entrust the Guggenheim Museum project to, she briefly considered Mendelsohn, who had come to live in the United States in 1941.

Once Rebay moved to the United States in 1927, after the success of her exhibition *Plastic Paintings: A New Medium by Hilla Rebay* at Marie Sterner's gallery, the baroness quickly entered the circles frequented by Irene Guggenheim, of whom she said: "She took me as a mother." In 1928, resuming the job that had allowed her to survive the hardship she had endured in Berlin just after the war, she painted a portrait of Solomon Guggenheim. "Convincing Guggenheim," then sixty-six years old, "to sit for a vivacious, witty, sophisticated European noblewoman cannot have been difficult. A great deal more persuasiveness was required to interest him seriously in the

painting of Bauer and Kandinsky, whom he did not know." It was Joan Lukach, Rebay's meticulous biographer, who gave this sly take on the meeting that, encouraged by Irene and her circle of friends, was the start of an exceptional friendship and intellectual rapport destined to last twenty-two years.

In 1928, Hilla worked on the English translation of Kandinsky's *Point and Line to Plane* while staying in touch with the Russian artist for whom, as his wife Nina recalled, New York was and would always be "a pretty little garden-city, a strange dream." In the meantime, she used her Manhattan studio to exhibit paintings by Bauer, Paul Klee, and Kandinsky, introducing their work to the sought-after world of potential collectors that she frequented. From New York she regularly informed Bauer of her activities and asked him to send her paintings both by him and by other artists she liked. In 1930, in conjunction with an exhibition devoted to her work at the Galerie Bernheim-Jeune, she traveled to Paris in the company of Irene and Solomon Guggenheim. As she began to think about the possibility of setting up a museum for their collection, she put the Guggenheims in touch with the world of Parisian artists. On that same occasion, Hilla arranged a trip to Dessau where, at the Bauhaus, the Guggenheims met Kandinsky and had the opportunity to acquire his 1923 *Composition 8* along with three other paintings.

The following year, during another trip through Europe, Rebay visited Das Geistreich in Berlin and once more went to Dessau, seeing Kandinsky again. In the meantime, László Moholy-Nagy, one of the baroness's closest friends, offered

Hilla Rebay in her studio in Connecticut at the end of the 1950s

Hilla Rebay, *Solomon Guggenheim*, 1928

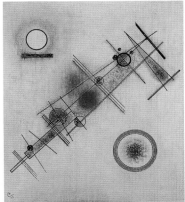

Wassily Kandinsky, *Composition 8 (Komposition 8)*, July 1923. Oil on canvas, 55⅛ x 79⅛ in. (140 x 201 cm). Solomon R. Guggenheim Museum, New York. Solomon R. Guggenheim Founding Collection, Gift, Solomon R. Guggenheim 37.262

Wassily Kandinsky, *Unstable*, November 1924. Watercolor, gouache, wash, india ink, and pencil on paper, 11½ x 10⅛ in. (29.3 x 25.7 cm). The Hilla von Rebay Foundation

Rudolf Bauer, *The Holy One (Red Point)*, 1936. Oil on canvas, 51⅜ x 51⅜ in. (130.5 x 130.5 cm). Solomon R. Guggenheim Museum, New York. Gift, Solomon R. Guggenheim, 37.170

his advice and helped strengthen her ties and those of the Guggenheims with Mondrian, Fernand Léger, Marc Chagall, Robert and Sonia Delaunay, Albert Gleizes, and others—leading to further acquisitions and to relationships that would endure.

By the end of 1930, the Guggenheim collection was considerable; it was not only his wife's wish that Solomon was satisfying when he gave Hilla the task of displaying a part of the collection in one of his suites at the Plaza Hotel in New York: once again Rebay put the spotlight on Bauer. At the start of 1931, growing more insistent and concerned about the future of Guggenheim's recent purchases, she wrote to Bauer that "the opening of the three *wonderful* rooms with the abstract art collection was a real sensation." Having similarly

reflected on the future of his collection, Solomon initially considered the possibility of transferring the works he possessed to the Metropolitan Museum of Art. However, like other collectors such as Gertrude Vanderbilt Whitney, Katherine Dreier, and Albert Gallatin, and as MoMA had already begun operations under the direction of Alfred H. Barr Jr., Guggenheim began to think seriously about founding a new museum. Rebay, returning to the translation of the expression *Gegenstandslos* used by Bauer, began to speak of it as a "Temple of Non-

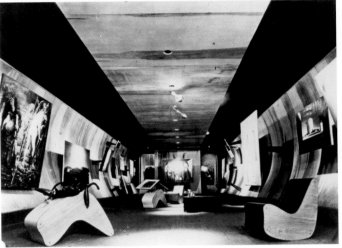

objectivity." Following a suggestion from Mondrian, in 1930
she considered entrusting the project to Frederick Kiesler, who
later, in 1942, set up the famous Art of This Century gallery
for Solomon's niece Peggy Guggenheim (who thought Hilla
a "witch"—the two harbored mutual dislike).

To compensate for bending the meaning of
Gegenstandslos in the course of translating it to English,
Rebay explained that "non-objectivity," a term used "for lack of
a better name" as Wright would caustically observe, "is the
religion of the future," maintaining that Bauer was "a genius,"
one of the "prophets" of a new spiritual life. By now a disciple

13   Solomon Guggenheim, Hilla Rebay

Max Ernst and Peggy Guggenheim in the
Surrealist gallery, Art of This Century,
New York, c. 1943

of this religion, "Guggi" (as Rebay and Bauer referred to
Solomon Guggenheim in their ongoing epistolary exchange)
had given her, de facto and starting in 1929, the task of
enriching and managing the collection. Relying heavily on
Bauer as an adviser and agent (as well as others, though to a
lesser extent), Rebay carried out her new role by acquiring the
works of artists whom she counted among the followers of
the new art, which she promoted by holding conferences,
cultivating select social relationships, and regularly traveling
to Europe over the course of the subsequent years.

In the 1930s, other ideas and opportunities developed
concerning the future of the growing Guggenheim collection.
In 1936, for example, in the course of developing Rockefeller
Center in mid-Manhattan, Nelson Rockefeller and Wallace
Harrison, one of the architects involved in the project, suggested
that Solomon build his Museum of Non-Objective Painting at
the Municipal Art Plaza planned between 52nd and 53rd
Streets; an underpass would link the intended location of the
Guggenheim collection to the new home of the Museum of
Modern Art to be built on 53rd Street. As we will see, the fact
that this proposal, which was under discussion as early as 1937
(and would re-emerge later), was not executed is symptomatic
of the situation, as was Barr's skepticism about it. Setting aside
the problem of the cost of the real estate, it is not unreasonable
to interpret this in light of the storied rivalry between Solomon
Guggenheim and the Rockefeller family, who were not only

involved in the gigantic construction venture of Rockefeller Center but who were also supporters of the initiatives carried out by MoMA—with Abby Aldrich Rockefeller as one of its founders, Barr its inspiration, and Rebay a critical witness.

In 1936, the Guggenheim collection was displayed at the Gibbes Memorial Art Gallery in Charleston, South Carolina, where the year before Rebay had held an exhibition of her own works. Irene and Solomon knew this city well; they had a residence there. Rebay's works were included in the exhibition, and the catalogue published for the occasion, *Solomon R. Guggenheim Collection of Non-Objective Paintings*, contained her essay "The Definition of Non-Objective Painting." This was the first of her attempts to define the meaning of non-objective art, or what she called "the great art tout-court which leads from materialistic to spiritual." Rebay asserts in this belated and somewhat naïve declamatory manifesto: "Because it is our destiny to be creative and our fate to become spiritual, humanity will come to develop and enjoy greater intuitive power through creations of great art, the glorious masterpieces of non-objectivity."

In February 1937, a year after the exhibition and four months before the Solomon R. Guggenheim Foundation was established with the aim (among others) of creating a museum to house the collection, the Philadelphia Art Alliance opened an exhibition accompanied by the *Second Enlarged Catalogue of the Solomon R. Guggenheim Collection of Non-Objective Paintings*. For a variety of reasons, which speak also to the causes of Rebay's difficulty in formulating a theoretical definition for non-objective art, the event stirred some tension between the protagonists of this story. Further proof that Hilla truly had trouble giving a balanced judgment of Bauer's work, as Herbert Read, the editor of *Burlington Magazine* from 1933 to 1938, had observed to her, the overwhelming number of works in the exhibition by Bauer, including the one serving as the catalogue's frontispiece, was likely to have incurred resentment among the other artists exhibited. Moreover, and this is the most telling point, Robert Delaunay and Kandinsky (accused by Rebay more than once of not sufficiently supporting Bauer's work) expressed to her, as curator of the exhibition, their disappointment with what she had written in the catalogue; both, though with different arguments, underlined her imprecise, generic application of the terms "abstract" and "non-objective," which she used almost interchangeably.

Kandinsky approached this matter punctiliously and, as he had explained on previous occasions, called Rebay's attention to a non-lexical discrepancy: "In your terminology, 'abstract' art operates with elements which have been 'abstracted' from some object. 'Non-objective' art creates its own elements, without making use of any object whatsoever. If this is the case, I do not understand why you term my paintings 'abstract,' since the Guggenheim collection has several of my paintings (even from the prewar era) which have nothing to do with an object. How am I to understand that?"

After these first steps in making the collection known, two years passed during which the number of works acquired by Guggenheim doubled, purchases made possible by the collapse of the art market in Germany and then by the Nazi regime's measures to dispose of works considered expressions of "degenerate art." Meanwhile, the effects of the 1929 economic collapse had to some extent (at least psychologically) abated, and the Guggenheim Foundation committed to establishing its own museum. When the decision was taken to found a Museum of Non-Objective Painting in New York, twelve years had elapsed since Rebay had painted Guggenheim's portrait. A demonstration of how their relationship had evolved in that time is seen when, in March 1939, Solomon Guggenheim informed her of his decision concerning the management of the museum. He specified that the foundation's trustees must "look to you as their authority and guide in all matters of non-objective art," and that "they do not wish, in any way, to restrict or limit you in your artistic work, either in the display of works of art, or in their selection, or in the development of their appreciation." Under Rebay's guidance, William Muschenheim realized the museum's interior design. Though he was born in New York City and studied at the Massachusetts Institute of Technology, Muschenheim belonged to the ranks of American architects who had earned Wright's disapproval by taking European architecture as their guiding light. In the 1920s, Muschenheim had studied with Peter Behrens in Vienna and went on to work in Berlin for Arthur Korn, who was a member of Der Ring and later one of the founders of London's Modern Architectural Research Group (MARS). This choice is surprising but not unjustified, as we will see; it points to a shift that will come in Rebay's thinking, being markedly different from the decision she would make five years on, in entrusting the construction of the Solomon R. Guggenheim Museum (as it became known in 1952) to Wright. In any case, Muschenheim designed the *Art of Tomorrow* exhibition to launch the activities of the Museum of Non-Objective Painting during the 1939 New York World's Fair, where Guggenheim planned to exhibit part of his collection in one of the pavilions.

On display at the Museum of Non-Objective Painting were 415 works selected from among more than 700 that made up the collection. Rebay edited the exhibition's catalogue, and, ignoring the past events involving Bauer described earlier, and the unkind attention they had generated, Rebay again gave him a preponderant role. Expressing an opinion that would remain unchanged over time, as attested in an interview in 1966, she felt that "also in this collection is represented the development of a genius, the greatest of all painters, spiritually the most advanced artist whose influence leads in the future. Rudolf Bauer, whose every work of Non-objectivity is an accomplished masterpiece."

The Museum of Non-Objective Painting was opened to the public on June 1, 1939, housed in a building at 24 East 54th Street in New York, a stone's throw from MoMA. The new MoMA building, designed by Philip Goodwin and Edward Durell Stone, despite Barr's opposition to the project had been inaugurated three weeks earlier. This physical and temporal proximity further fomented the rivalry that had dogged, from the very beginning, the two leading New York museums of contemporary art. And this antagonism was not simply latent—it was openly demonstrated, for example, by the way in which Rebay spoke of the Museum of Modern Art well before 1939. On one occasion in 1930, just a few months after MoMA was founded, Rebay wrote to Bauer: "There is a 'new museum' and though not yet a building, it owns pictures already, and exhibitions take place in a private apartment, called 'new museum.' So there were now bad Klees, Braques, Matisses, and Picassos, among others, rather mixed, and all financed by my Mrs. Rockefeller."

Rebay had a low opinion of what was being hatched in the incubator of MoMA, and she made it absolutely clear. Returning to the subject on March 31, 1931, Hilla informed Bauer that "the Barr," not known to be an admirer of Bauer, "who is Director of the new museum wants to do an international abstract exhibition on one floor of a skyscraper which is known as the 'new museum.' It is sponsored by wealthy people and is always very crowded. They had also wanted to borrow Kandinsky and watercolors by you from Guggi and me, but I said: refuse, that is no company for you."

Chapter Three
The Tyranny of the Skyscraper

From 1943, Wright grew increasingly aware of the innate dangers in the unspoken but mutual animosity his patrons harbored for the Museum of Modern Art, which was under the leadership of Alfred H. Barr Jr. Even when Wright had just started working for Solomon Guggenheim, he took up the matter with insistence. We will return to these considerations later. For now, considering the reasons for Wright's heated confrontation with James Johnson Sweeney after 1952 (when the latter rose to become director of the Guggenheim Museum after serving as head of MoMA's Department of Painting and Sculpture), it seems that Wright's concerned tones in discussing the matter with Hilla Rebay as early as 1943 were not so much a premonition as a lucid interpretation of established facts, events that had already happened, as Hilla's earlier letters to Bauer indicate.

Thus, when Wright laid out the opportunities he had identified for proceeding to acquire a site for the new museum, he took care to inform Rebay that "the feeling grows on me that to tie in closely with the MoMA might be a mistake—even if we wanted to put the extra money into the property. We might fall in competition. . . . The MoMA is already dated in so many respects." Though the most striking passage in the letter is the one on the cost of the site—a lot on West 54th Street that Rebay thought suitable in part because of its proximity to the Museum of Non-Objective Painting, housed in a former showroom at 24 East 54th Street—it is the last few words which deserve our attention: "The MoMA is already dated in so many respects." The statement shows clearly that Wright believed the processes by which the project Barr had announced in 1929 was being carried out to be passé. Barr had studied with Paul J. Sachs, one of the founders of MoMA, whose courses at Harvard had dealt with museum management. Having absorbed Sachs's teachings, Barr shared them with other young minds who like himself and Philip Johnson (his friend, fellow student, and traveling companion) were Harvard educated. And this background clarifies why Barr aimed for the new museum "to establish a very fine collection of the immediate ancestors, American and European, of the modern movement"; his objective was to organize the museum according to an idealized model of the Bauhaus.

In an unusual display of restraint, Wright defined the project as being "already dated"; however, he actually opposed it, though for different reasons than Rebay. His disapproval was also justified by the choices made by MoMA: in 1932 and in 1938, respectively, the museum put on the exhibitions *Modern Architecture: International Exhibition* and *Bauhaus, 1919–1928*, which exalted Germany's cultural contribution to the development of modern architecture, de facto relegating Wright to the position of "dated ancestor." Even Rebay had thought this, before her opinions changed radically in 1943—another demonstration of the breadth and depth of the paradoxes that are woven into the fabric of this story.

Having said this, to return to the thread of events we must note that four years separate the inauguration day of the Museum of Non-Objective Painting from June 1, 1943, when Rebay wrote her first letter to Wright informing him of her intention to entrust to him the project of constructing a building, though not defining the type of construction. "I need a fighter, a lover of space, an originator, a tester and a wise man," Hilla wrote, asking Wright to design not a museum but rather "a temple of spirit, a monument" for the Guggenheim collection. Likely thinking of the earlier exhibitions at MoMA, Rebay clarified, citing a less than apt example (the Einstein Tower built by Mendelsohn in Potsdam between 1919 and 1922) that "functionalism does not agree with non-objectivity." While it seems that in 1943 Rebay was unaware that Wright was still fully active, the latter thought that the writer of the letter addressed to him seven days before his seventy-sixth birthday was a man. Despite the misunderstandings, which demonstrate how far apart they were, Wright soon afterward met Guggenheim and Rebay in New York. "I would love to see Taliesin," the baroness wrote on June 14, but "it would take too long time to arrange"; she explained further, sharing with Wright her constant worry, "Mr. Guggenheim is 82 years old and we have no time to lose."

Guggenheim and Rebay put forward their needs to Wright regarding their different ambitions and their shared goals: Hilla, enthusiastic and equipped with a good deal of rhetoric, spoke on several occasions (taking up Bauer's lexicon) of a "temple," a "church," a "sanctuary," or a "monument"; Solomon, with a more elite vision, imagined a "house," open to the public and as noble as the ones he regularly visited. Both, however, ruled out the desire to build a museum; rather, they imagined a place suitable to welcome an artistic community and to educate the public, sharing the conviction that non-objective art could only be appreciated in unusual spaces, an environment that enhances spirituality, conceived to favor the fulfilment of a maieutic method. As we have seen, Hilla called Wright an "originator," believing that the works of art that she had helped collect represented "a new beginning," in which the architect needed to involve the public and artists, designing an architectural organism that was just as innovative and fully "consecrated" to the task.

As we have seen, Solomon ("the only bible [Rebay] ever knew," according to Wright) had entrusted her with executing decisions on behalf of the foundation. His confidence explains why, probably on the advice of Irene Guggenheim, she first approached Wright. Hilla in fact, before receiving this suggestion, had spoken of the project with Edmund Körner, who in Germany had designed, among other projects, the Essen synagogue and the extension of the Folkwang Museum in Hagen; she may have spoken with Ludwig Mies van der Rohe as well. (In a curious coincidence, Mies used a photograph of a painting by Kandinsky that belonged to Solomon Guggenheim to compose a collage of a project presentation for a museum in a small city.) Around the time when they decided to commission Wright to construct the "temple of non-objectivity," Rebay once again asked Frederick Kiesler for his opinion, and it was probably he who informed her of Solomon's decision to hand over the management of the foundation to her. Although Kiesler was himself out of the running on account of having designed Peggy Guggenheim's Art of This Century gallery the previous year, he clearly had the talent and necessary experience to "organize a space for the great masterpieces of our collection," as Hilla desired. Evidence of this can be found in Kiesler's numerous projects of continuous structures, such as that of a spiral-shaped department store in 1925, and the arrangement of "endless spaces" such as the *Raumbühne*, which he prepared in 1924 for the *Internationale Ausstellung neuer Theatertechnik* in Vienna; these works, for various reasons to which we will return later, call for a comparison with Wright's post-1943 designs for the Guggenheim.

At the same time, however, Rebay sought counsel from her old friend László Moholy-Nagy, who, after having left first Germany and then England, moved to Chicago in 1937 and there founded the New Bauhaus. He had been among the most brilliant teachers of the school established by Walter Gropius, was an artist appreciated by Solomon Guggenheim, and was a trusted adviser of the baroness. In May 1943, he sent a carefully constructed list that was anything but banal of possible candidates for the role Rebay was getting ready to assign for the new museum (which Hilla was still describing as a "temple," "church," and other colorful names). In the letter, transcribed by Joan Lukach, Moholy-Nagy names (in addition to himself): Walter Gropius, Richard Neutra, Marcel Breuer, Mart Stam, William Lescaze, Werner Moser, Paul Nelson, William Humby, George Keck, Le Corbusier, and Alvar Aalto (the last two suggestions are useful to keep in mind for what we will see later). Curiously, though the list is broad, it is missing Wright, as well as Erich Mendelsohn, and especially Mies van der Rohe. The absence of Mies's name on this list is as unexpected as it is telling: Mies's Tugendhat House had been featured on the cover of the catalogue for MoMA's 1932 exhibition *Modern Architecture*, curated by Henry-Russell Hitchcock and Philip Johnson. Two years earlier, Johnson had entrusted the interior design of his own apartment (in the same building in which the Barrs lived) to the director of the Bauhaus at the time and to Lilly Reich; the results were documented in the book *The International Style*. Wright, for his part, had no doubts about linking the architects who belonged to the German artistic circles to which Hilla had ties, and whom she had helped and supported after 1933, to those of Gropius, Le Corbusier, and Breuer—to whom he acidly referred as "left wing modernists." To him they represented an invading presence, as he would write some time later to Dutch architect Hendrik Th. Wijdeveld on October 21, 1947 (who twenty-two years prior had devoted three famous issues of the journal *Wendingen* to Wright and in 1931 had organized in Amsterdam the first European venue of Wright's international exhibition). Wright's letter reproaches Wijdeveld for agreeing with those who did not give him full credit for his role as pioneer of modern archi-tecture—which had also emerged in MoMA's early exhibitions on architecture. "The breach between myself and these men has widened," states Wright, rejecting Wijdeveld's request to join him at Taliesin. "They think, speak and work in two

dimensions while idealizing the third and vice versa. I feel that I
am far beyond them now as I was in 1910 and their apostasy
has only served to betray the cause of an organic architecture
in the nature of materials which I believe to be the architecture
of Democracy."

Having overcome Rebay's understandable uncertainties
and apprehensions, on June 29, 1943, Guggenheim (then
eighty-two) commissioned Wright, who was six years his junior,
to design the museum. The contract states that the architect's
task was to develop the project, as well as, oddly, to select the
site where the building was to be situated. The overall costs of
the project, including that of buying the land, was not to exceed
$1 million. (In 1946 the projected costs rose to $1.5 million, and
three years later, in his will, Solomon set aside $2 million for
the building alone; construction ended up costing around $3.5
million by its completion in 1959.) Furthermore, the contract
provides a clause that would automatically terminate the
contracting parties' obligations if the construction site was not
purchased within a year of signing. Without knowing exactly
where to build it, Wright began to work on both the project and
at the same time the choice of a site.

It was not until March 1944 that the decision to acquire
a lot at Fifth Avenue and the south corner of 89th Street was
confirmed. After a final real estate transaction carried out by the
Solomon R. Guggenheim Foundation in 1951, the area reached
the dimensions of the lot on which the museum now stands.
Before this third purchase was completed, in 1948, the Museum
of Non-Objective Painting was transferred to the adjacent
townhouse at 1071 Fifth Avenue, acquired in 1946. Here the
museum stayed provisionally until 1956, and its layout was once
again designed by Muschenheim, who not without reason felt
he was a good candidate for the task entrusted to Wright.

The search for a building site followed a circuitous path,
north to the Bronx and back to Manhattan. During the course
of 1943, Wright began the search, advised and guided by
Robert Moses, a distant cousin (though this did not make him
an uncritical supporter of the architect's proposals). "Cousin
Bob" was the omnipotent Parks Commissioner, and much more
besides, in New York City, from the 1920s to the 1960s; he
knew the real estate market like no one else and was capable
of bringing to life public works involving significant investment,
earning the title of "America's greatest builder." Wright sifted
through the various options, following Moses's not entirely

Solomon Guggenheim and Frank Lloyd
Wright in New York, 1945

Robert Moses with the model of the Battery Park Bridge, New York, 1939

McCarren Pool, New York, July 12, 1937. Robert Moses, Commissioner of the Department of Parks, during the New Deal developed the plan for the pool-building project in New York, financed by the Works Progress Administration.

innocent advice—he considered Moses "a splendid fellow and powerful," and Guggenheim felt he was "a man who has the interests of the city at heart." On July 14, 1943, Wright informed his client that the most suitable decision was to acquire a site north of Manhattan, about eight acres in size, and costing about $250,000, at the Henry Hudson Memorial Park in Riverdale in the Bronx, facing the Hudson River. "Now," he wrote to Guggenheim, "in the Moses view (and it is my own view), this is a break from the old museum tradition," since the choice he advocated would have allowed "the chance to create a truly creative group of buildings in the heart of Greater New York, embracing gardens and attractive courts, each containing a group of art works according to their nature." The weighing of possibilities continued, bringing to focus three crucial considerations capable of supporting it. The new museum, immersed in nature, in Wright's words would be "a genuine relief from the cinder heap old New York is bound to become," and it would be easily accessible to visitors since "helicopter and motor travel will become quite universal after the war." Moreover, "according to Mr. Moses, the great population trend is to the Eastside, just opposite to the pro-posed site—but the high class improvements will cling to the stream-lined highway and the Hudson." If the choice fell on the Riverdale area, Wright continued, the decision would only serve to confirm that "you have been a pioneer always, Mr. Guggenheim. So has your Curator, Hilla Rebay. So have I, your architect. Why stop now? There is a momentous decision to be made."

This letter brings light again to the role Moses played in suggesting what might have been the best site for the new museum, but above all it implies that the reasons for which Wright considered the spot in the Riverdale park preferable above all others, and illustrated this clearly to Guggenheim, were not at all contingent. It is not only the reference to helicopters and automobiles—the means of transportation that Wright felt would guarantee mobility in the future—that shows his 1943 letter to be perfectly congruent with the ideas behind the urban planning concepts that he had been developing since the late 1920s. Those ideas, as Neil Levine has demonstrated, were formed in logical comparison with the (more or less contemporary) ideas expressed by Le Corbusier. What Wright had thought about the future of the city in the age of mechanization was translated into a series of articles and conferences, and later in his project for Broadacre City. The latter was formalized in 1935, when a grand model of the whole dispersed city was displayed at Rockefeller Center. Among the characteristics of Broadacre, conceived as a radical alternative to "the city, as we know today, [which] is destined to die," there were those that Wright defined as "objectives," aimed to serve as catalysts of movements enabled by means of transportation and the new modes of communication for a population spread "in the country," calculating 2.5 inhabitants per acre. It is easy to imagine Wright thinking that the Guggenheim Museum, if built far from central Manhattan in a park by the Hudson, might represent one of his "automobile objectives," such as "the planetarium" (a revealing example as we shall soon see) or "the great concert hall, museums and art galleries" that "will be developed to gratify what is natural and desirable in the get-together instinct of the community" in a city where, as Mumford wrote, "Mechanization Takes Command."

The words cited above come from the well-known talk titled "The City," one of the six Kahn Lectures Wright gave at Princeton University in 1930. This lecture offers a useful summary of the ideas and main inspirations for the Broadacre project and helps explain why Wright considered the Riverdale park the most suitable site for Guggenheim's museum. Soon enough, however, this option was abandoned, and the museum's destiny grew more precise, while the decision to build in Manhattan matured, "changing our idea of a building from horizontal to perpendicular," as Wright put it to Rebay in December 1943. Despite the obvious conclusions, this radical change of address does not mean that the Guggenheim Museum we know was the fruit of a similarly extreme abandonment of the ideas expressed by Wright in the Kahn Lectures, and the source of the plan dear to Wright of building the museum far from Manhattan. "The City," his final lecture in the Kahn series, built further on his diagnosis—"the apotheosis of landlord"—made in the lecture that preceded it, titled "The Tyranny of the Skyscraper"; there he spoke of the skyscraper as "the congestion promoter . . . a mechanical conflict of machine resources . . . that opposes and kills the automobile's contribution to the city." Wright judged New York to be "piled high and piling higher into the air," the cradle of this form of tyranny, and Manhattan "a forest of riveted steel posts, riveted girder beams, riveted brackets and concrete slabs, steel reinforced, closed in by heavy brick and stone walls, all carried by steel framing." He continued, saying "the true nature of this thing is prostitute to the shallow picturesque, in attempt to render a wholly insignificant, therefore inconsequential, beauty. In any depth of human experience it is an ignoble sacrifice."

After having read the Kahn Lectures and observing the Guggenheim Museum today, it is not difficult to understand how this construction was conceived and so obstinately desired by Wright as a response to the various manifestations of what he called "betrayal of democracy," which in New York City was exacerbated by the rules governing the real estate market, the customary ways in which buildings were constructed, the prevalence of the "picturesque," and the spread of the cult of the "insignificant." Surrounded by this thicket, the Guggenheim stands out thanks to the heterodoxy of its unchanging and constructive conception and the originality that shaped its unique form. This form, with unequalled rhetoric, achieves its own "fated" function of "defin[ing] the limits of the immaterial" and "set[ting] a limit around a substance which otherwise would dissolve like air in the All," to borrow the words of György Lukács.

Chapter Four
Wright's Monument

Though he did not abandon hope that Solomon Guggenheim would personally visit the Riverdale lot, in July 1943 Wright told Hilla Rebay, "if finally Mr. Guggenheim should prefer to leave his mark within the center of present New York City, I think the Park Avenue sites Moses suggested are both excellent." And he continued, once again making a loaded reference to MoMA: "Our installation will have drawing power wherever we plant it because [it] will be organic in character and truly exemplar . . . quite enough to make everybody mad including the MoMA especially. They have nothing of this kind." Almost at the same time, when the project had taken shape, Wright declared that he preferred one of the two areas suggested by Moses, situated between Madison Avenue and 36th Street, close to the Morgan Library, rather than the lot facing Park Avenue between 69th and 70th Streets, considered in the meantime.

As it was, the possibility entertained of building at the city limits, far from Manhattan, it seems, did not translate into any plan. Wright's earlier experiences, from which he drew in launching his work on the project between mid-1943 and the start of the following year, involved very different develop-ments, congruent with the resolution to build the museum on a lot that was bounded by the grid of Manhattan's streets—though for the time being, the architect could only guess as to the characteristics and location of the site, both of which carried equal importance, even though for him their specifics were ultimately irrelevant.

In arranging the project, Wright took inspiration from works he had designed earlier—both built and those that remained on paper—which deserve to be noted here. Keeping in mind the fact that Rebay believed that diffuse light and no stairs were the essential features for the museum, Wright thought he could fulfill the first requirement by turning to a solution he had already tested, though with less than satis-factory results from the practical point of view. In particular, he thought of using—and refining—the construction technique that had allowed him to benefit from the natural light and transparency of convex hulls, to create unusual and highly

S. C. Johnson & Son Administration
Building, Racine, Wisconsin, 1936–39.
Loading test of a column prototype
(Frank Lloyd Wright in the foreground).
View of the interior of a skylight built out
of Pyrex glass tubes. View of the Great
Workroom skylight under construction
(workmen installing Pyrex glass tubes)

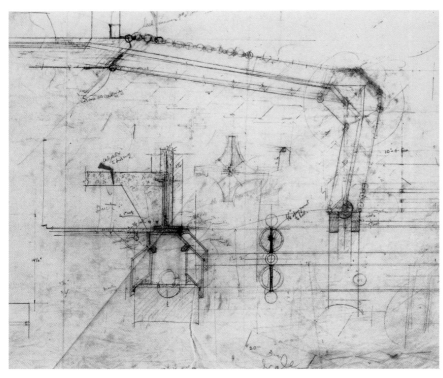

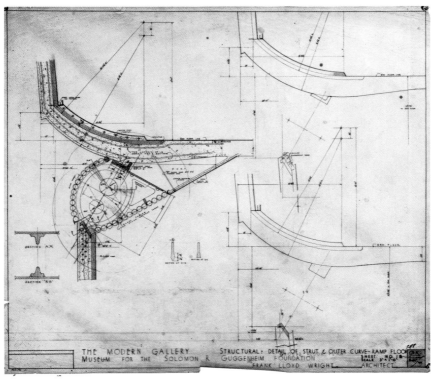

THE MODERN GALLERY   STRUCTURAL: DETAIL OF STRUT & OUTER CURVE~RAMP FLOOR
MUSEUM FOR THE SOLOMON R GUGGENHEIM FOUNDATION
                        FRANK LLOYD WRIGHT   ARCHITECT

S. C. Johnson & Son Administration Building, Racine, Wisconsin, 1936–39. Drawing of skylights using Pyrex glass tubes

Guggenheim Museum. Structural detail drawing of the ramp's strut and the skylight's glass tubes. The drawing bears Solomon Guggenheim's initials at lower right.

captivating effects in one of his greatest works, the S. C. Johnson & Son Administration Building in Racine, Wisconsin, finished in 1939. In this building, which Guggenheim and Rebay knew, Wright had put forward a new and undisputable proof of his bold creativity in conceiving the structure and of his inventive and nonchalant experimentalism in fine-tuning the elements of construction. In addition to the unparalleled and highly original dendriform columns, guaranteeing unimaginable stability with their treelike shape, the lilypads formed the shell of the volume that held the offices; for the interiors of the Johnson Administration Building, Wright relied on spatial configurations defined by exterior balustrades, continuous and wrapped bands, and the translucency of the envelope. In this way he employed a formal repertory directly comparable with what he used later in the Guggenheim. Moreover, he chose glass tubes manufactured by the Corning Glass Works Co., mainly employed in the chemical and pharmaceutical industries, for the external shell and roofing. Maximizing and taking advantage of its features in an unusual way, Wright also used the material to create the rounded skylights inserted between the brickwork and the roof, along the upper area of the perimeter of the building. The working plans for this band of glass in L-shaped sections form the most direct precedent for the laborious study Wright dedicated to the Guggenheim's skylights, with which he intended to allow natural light to permeate, suffusing the building as Rebay had requested, preoccupied as she was from the very start with the project's museographic implications.

Wright's letter of October 8, 1943, to his Racine client Hibbard Johnson leaves no doubt about this and shows how, from the moment Wright received the commission to design the Guggenheim, he intended to reuse the technique employed in Racine. The letter was a reply to Johnson's message of October 4 informing Wright that he was determined to commission him to build the tower for the new research laboratories for his industrial complex. In communicating this decision, Hib Johnson also expressed the wish that this new plan not lead to "a financial and construction nightmare" as happened during and after the construction of the office building, completed four years before. If we consider that the main issue in construction terms behind Johnson's worries was precisely those glass tubes used in cladding the skylights, through which rain poured, it is not difficult to appreciate the skill, arrogance, and determination rising from Wright's inconstantly logical reply sent by post to his generous client. There he reassured Johnson by letting him know his resolution and quoting eloquently the name of Solomon Guggenheim: "We are using the technique developed getting that baby born [the Administration Building in Racine] (tubes, mastic, etc.) to build a great million dollar building on Madison Avenue next the Morgan Library—a Museum (not a morgue) to house the Guggenheim Collection— you will see what you shall see."

The plans for the Johnson Wax laboratories and those for the Guggenheim were thus developed in parallel, though the Racine complex was completed nine years before the museum. The two buildings are expressions of analogous structural conceptions, drawn out in opposite directions. In the Racine complex, the laboratories are set within a tall, slender tower with rounded corners that is subdivided into fifteen floors, including the lobby. The floor slabs alternate between squares with rounded angles and circular ones and are supported by a thin central core, a solution that could be compared with the one invented by Frederick Kiesler for his spiral-shaped department store scheme (1925). Consequently, the floors with a circular slab, having a diameter that is smaller than the square slab below it, are not attached to the shell made up of bent glass tubes laid out horizontally. Thus the whole structure exhibits spatial effects and visual permeability thanks to the linear projection of the floor slabs; this is similar to the Guggenheim, which is however more radical, as the structure is also cantilevered but is not flat, being mostly conceived as a continuous, wrapped, spiral beam.

In completing the Johnson Research Tower, Wright experimented with a solution that derives even more directly from the one he was working on for the Guggenheim, as can be confirmed by the fact that the analogies one can draw in examining his two greatest works, conceived in the same years, are the fruit of reciprocal exchanges. At the Racine complex, Wright inserted a structure next to the tower housing the laboratories as the reception area for the advertising department, where he also built, in addition to an elegant glass backdrop, a surprising and light translucid cupola. This low cupola is supported by a continuous structural frame of metal circles of decreasing diameters converging on the central eye; the surfaces of both the circles and the eye are made of tangential Pyrex tubes. Having carried out the experiment, Wright was

Guggenheim Museum. Plan and section of the glass dome, variation of 1954–55

Johnson Research Tower, Racine, Wisconsin, 1943–50, reception area of the advertising department

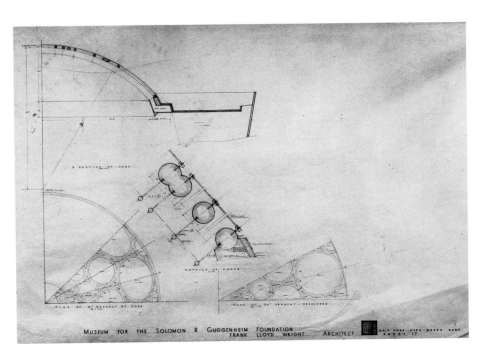

MUSEUM FOR THE SOLOMON R GUGGENHEIM FOUNDATION
FRANK LLOYD WRIGHT ARCHITECT

Gordon Strong Automobile Objective and Planetarium, Sugarloaf Mountain, Maryland, 1924. View and plan sketches

Gordon Strong Automobile Objective and Planetarium. Section drawing

Guggenheim Museum. Elevation drawing showing a red exterior, 1943–44

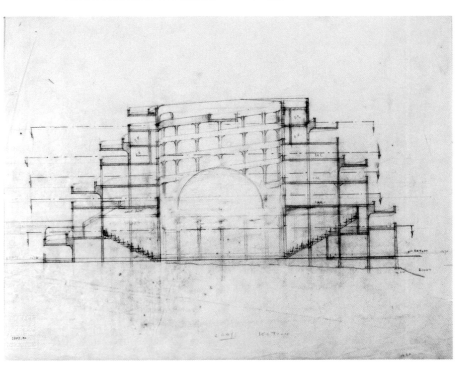

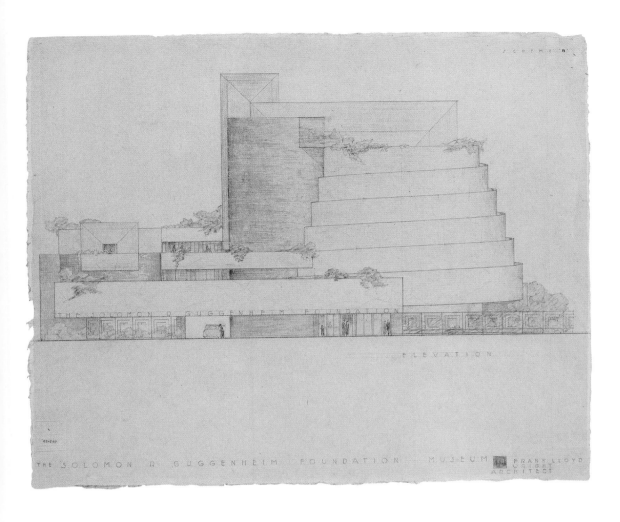

THE SOLOMON D GUGGENHEIM FOUNDATION

ELEVATION

THE SOLOMON R GUGGENHEIM FOUNDATION MUSEUM FRANK LLOYD WRIGHT ARCHITECT

able to fine-tune an architectural device that he had studied for the Guggenheim, which would undergo various reworkings over the subsequent years, in the course of the plans he was preparing for the museum's dome. Carrying on with his experiments on solutions he dreamed up for the museum, Wright also tested (for less challenging conditions) a combination of a different version of the glass roof with a winding ramp at the Morris Gift Shop in San Francisco, a refined and intimate space. There, Wright was able to employ the skills of his son-in-law William Wesley Peters in constructing this building between 1948 and 1950, during the same years when the Johnson Research Tower was being completed.

For his work on the Guggenheim, Wright especially favored as a model a project from twenty years earlier: the Gordon Strong Automobile Objective and Planetarium on Sugarloaf Mountain in Maryland, worked on between 1924 and 1925 but never built. For this project, the architect took a determined approach to the spiral theme, though in Maryland he had treated the structure more canonically than at the Guggenheim, designing a building with a circular floor plan from which rose a continuous coil supported by pillars. The diameter of the spiral, like Fermat's, progressively and uniformly narrowed toward the top, crowned in one version of the project by an antenna placed in the center of the roof level, between two loops. The building, shaped in this way, was supposed to wrap around a space with a cupola intended to house the planetarium (though the space would serve rather more prosaic functions than the one in the New York museum). In the Maryland planetarium, the spiral is shorn of the meanings it traditionally possessed, interpreted in a secular and free way as the symbol of faith in progress, or one of the "automobile objectives" spread across the land which Wright would later specify, as we saw, in his lecture "The City." This spiral was intended to allow visitors to reach the pinnacle of the building by car and enjoy the view of the surrounding landscape.

Wright's decision to give the Guggenheim Museum the shape of an upturned ziggurat was reached rapidly, but the economic restrictions in his contract, the foreseeable construction difficulties, the way in which the configuration of the area was defined and then changed, the collection's growth, the public's hostility, and finally the variation in the functional plan would bring more laborious and complex adjustments and compromises, adopted as the years passed, gradually contributing to molding the architecture we now admire. Concerning the evolution of the functional plan, we must remember that between 1948 and 1949 the Solomon R. Guggenheim Foundation bought the works collected by the German gallery owner Karl Nierendorf, active in New York from 1937, around 730 pieces including about 121 by Paul Klee, and those belonging to Herwarth Walden's widow, Nell, equally important but less numerous. This represented a marked turning point for the collection's makeup, which was destined to grow steadily in the subsequent years.

Furthermore, better to understand the perpetual change in circumstances Wright had to face in preparing his plans, we should recall that less than three years after Solomon's death, in 1952, Rebay resigned from the director-ship of the foundation. Harry Guggenheim, a nephew of Solomon's and later president of the foundation's board, would become Wright's main interlocutor, proving himself a more pragmatic, decisive client, tuned in to public opinion and prudent in a way that Hilla never was. Rebay, moreover, had been influenced by Bauer and Moholy-Nagy, whom Wright bitterly disliked, during the years in which she was personally in charge of the museum project. These circum-stances shed light on why she appeared to be constantly undecided in the face of her architect's heterodox choices. "While I have no doubt that your building will be a great monument to yourself," Rebay told Wright in 1945 and again in 1946 (thus foreshadowing Mumford's assessment fourteen years later, which we have already quoted), "I cannot visualize how much (or how little) it will do for paintings. . . . We need a monument to painting also which is our main interest. . . . We do not want the paintings to be overlooked by the visitors, who otherwise might see only a glorious building." The accusation was explicit, and having being charged several times with conceiving the building as a monument built for his own glory, Wright, deaf to Hilla's requests to take a more "humble and less arrogant" attitude, hit back with: "And what is this inimical fury over 'the monument to myself'? Silly. Silly! . . . I need no monument anyway. What is the work this building is supposed to do? If it doesn't do that work superbly well, then what is the building to me?" Likewise, to his client's worry about the secondary place that the paintings would have with respect to the spatial configuration Wright was planning, he replied bluntly: "The fact is, modern painting of the non-objective type has been out of place in the orthodox environment. Only as our cause in architecture wins can your cause in painting win."

It is clear that from the moment in which he began to work with Hilla and elaborate the first ideas for the project, confirming the general ambiguity of the baroness's emphatic declarations about the plans, Wright constantly and resoundingly had to reassure her that his proposals would satisfy the requirements for the public's enjoyment of the works in the Guggenheim collection. As excerpts from their correspondence show, by 1945 Wright had already seen how, despite the growing friendship between them, Rebay's initial enthusiasm from two years earlier had begun to waver. As a result, Wright believed that her doubts were nourished, above all, by the advice given to her by her "European" associates. To confront this situation, which had evolved to the point where Hilla was considering involving Mies van der Rohe in the project, Wright made a proposal which for him was both unusual and unexpected. While he was in an intense phase of the work, in March 1945, Wright sent a letter to Rebay that was a small masterpiece of clever rhetoric. In the letter he aimed to provoke the baroness by suggesting that he supported an encounter with some "consultants," to whom he would submit his plans for their judgment. His tone was insinuating, and rightly so; he skillfully countered Rebay's cherished notion of bringing in Mies van der Rohe, offering to augment the number of consultants using a suffusive rhetorical tactic: "Beside Mies there are a number of German refugee-architects like Mendelsohn, Behrendt, Breuer, Gropius and several others, all fairly capable." Having said this, he added with a lightly dismissive tone: "They would cost the Foundation nothing if I managed it. I could invite them all in together, show them the plans and invite their criticism if you would feel any easier in your mind toward your responsibilities. Think about this." The move and the parrying brought about mixed results, and Wright would continue to consider the German architects who had emigrated to the United States in the 1930s as his main adversaries concerning the museum project. This conviction, which would become stronger over time, brought him into bitter conflict even with Henry-Russell Hitchcock, one of his great admirers, who in 1942 helped publicize his work by publishing *In the Nature of Materials: The Buildings of Frank Lloyd Wright, 1887–1941*. Linking him sarcastically with Gropius, "[who] is a scientist, not an architect nor an artist, so you are an historian, not an interpreter nor an artist," in the 1950s he accused Hitchcock of being a partisan (as he complied with MoMA) of those he derided as the "Bauhausers," or "left wing modernists," of whom Wright had spoken so hostilely, as we have seen, to Wijdeveld in 1947. Thus, making an implicit but clear reference to the exhibitions organized by MoMA in the field of architecture, Wright yet again highlighted his conviction that "Hitchcock and Johnson" were to be included among the most determined supporters of the dangerous adversaries of his project for the Guggenheim Museum, the Bauhausers. "As Bauhaus propaganda goes (now), the day of the great Architect in America is over, if the Bauhausers can manage," he wrote to Hitchcock on February 18, 1953. "We Americans now, by way of Hitchcock and Johnson, sell ourselves to European standardizations and team work of plan factories when the great Architecture of the individual free should really be our concern. . . . Meantime, go see the 'corkscrew museum': Bauhaus epithet of the neophyte Drexler to help me to build the new Museum. This word for the opus shows how much the Bauhaus really wants to see the building built."

Chapter Five
Designing the Guggenheim

In the final weeks of 1943, Wright began the first draft of his proposal for the project—which was destined to come to a close only after six reworkings—amidst the growing turmoil that would accompany the construction of the Guggenheim Museum during its entire course. This first draft was the beginning of a story best summed up by Erasmus's adage that "what is valuable is usually of difficult acquisition and things that are beautiful are hard to come by."

From the beginning, Wright was determined that the museum not become "a morgue"—a term he used for New York's Metropolitan Museum of Art—and at the same time was concerned by the slowness with which the decision on the purchase of the site was progressing; Solomon Guggenheim was inclined to postpone any decisions, as he anticipated a decline in the real estate market after the end of the war, despite having some apprehension about the time the project would require in order to be brought to completion. To overcome Solomon's hesitation, Wright informed him on December 31, 1943, that he wished to submit some drawings to him; one would think that he had first showed them to Hilla Rebay, since he had prepared them toward the end of 1943. Wright adopted a technique that was unusual for him, making a series of water-color perspectives (likely executed by Peter Berndtson) which present different versions of a building on a site presumably facing Madison Avenue. It was probably on the recommendation of Olgivanna Milanov, Wright's wife since 1928, that two of the images were shown to Guggenheim in March 1944, when the purchase of the lot on Fifth Avenue was either imminent or had just been completed. Both images show perspectives of an upturned spiral, composed of five coils, intended to house the display galleries. The spirals grow tighter toward the bottom, demonstrating that the building's characteristics did not undergo substantial changes over the fifteen years that elapsed between when the images were presented and the museum's opening. Moreover—a further proof of how the earliest proposals

for the project presented a compositional strategy that was
destined to remain stable—in both watercolors, where there are
some inconsequential variations in the details, the main body
(for which various colors had been imagined) was indifferently
placed either to the left or right of the principal facade.

Conceptually, all the designs prepared between the
summer of 1943 and the start of 1944 respond to a consistent
interpretation of the functional plan. They offer a single configuration with regard to the direction of the exhibition path and the
lighting criteria, and the same scheme concerning the structuring of the volumes lined up along a continuous plane, raised
and extended along the length of the main facade. On the
floating pedestal, two volumes of different heights rise upward,
variously connected and joined to accommodate both the
galleries distributed around a dilated, empty atrium illuminated
from above (the "crystal court") and the "Holy of Holies," the
space where the collection's most important works are displayed (now called the "High Gallery"). An auditorium has been
located in the basement, with the idea of placing reclining seats
to allow visitors to view projections on the curved ceiling, as at a
planetarium; the smaller volume, on the other hand, holds
spaces that are more fragmented and would be used for various
functions. It is useful to dwell on the latter, as it helps make
clear the patrons' expectations and the aims they pursued.

In addition to strictly technical rooms, this lateral
volume's distributive layout, later termed the "Monitor," provided space for studies and offices, an apartment for Rebay,
and a larger vaulted area, arranged to allow artists to carry out
audio and visual experiments, called the "Ocular Chamber." The
idea of equipping the museum with such a space—which
moved as the project was reworked with respect to the spiral—
was later abandoned; nevertheless, it was the logical product of
Rebay's attempt, from the beginning of the 1930s, to bring to
life a Guggenheim Film Center, in competition with MoMA.
The objective of including it in the museum was to support the
research carried out in experimental cinematography, which
Hilla had enjoyed in Berlin on seeing the films of Hans Richter
and Viking Eggeling, both connected to the journal *G*, edited by
Mies van der Rohe—"Mies the ruler," Wright called him sarcastically. Toward this end, in the 1945 version of the project for
the new museum, Wright studied the configuration of the
Ocular Chamber, consulting with Oskar Fischinger. While still
in Germany prior to immigrating to the United States at the

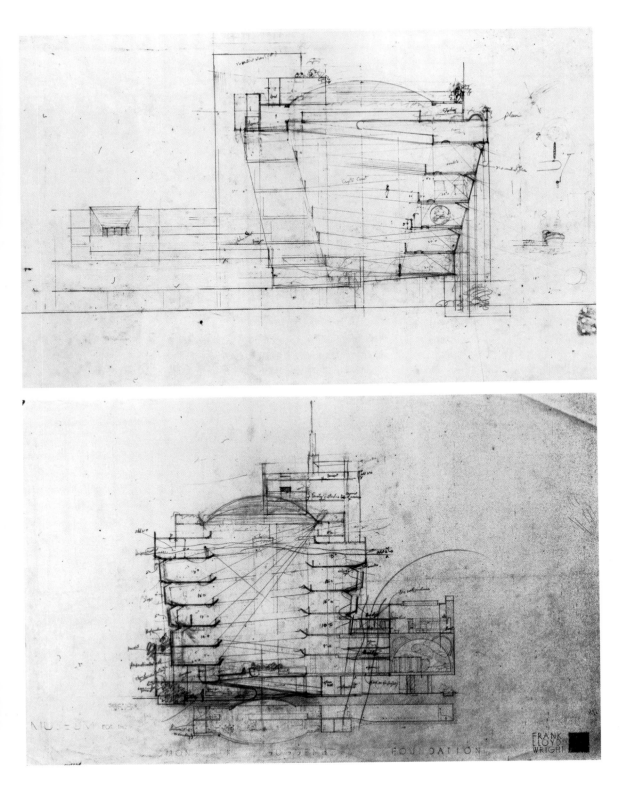

end of the 1920s, without abandoning his own career as painter, Fischinger had carried on the research of Walter Ruttmann, creator of one of the masterpieces of avant-garde cinematography, the 1927 *Berlin—Symphony of a Metropolis*. Fischinger made seven experimental films, *Studie 6–12*, between 1928 and 1930, following in the footsteps of Ruttmann's *Opus 1–5*, filmed between 1923 and 1926. Moreover, he had developed cameras and carried out experiments projecting multiple images, drawing the attention of Fritz Lang, who employed him in making his 1928 film *Frau im Mod*. Fischinger's intent, which Rebay admired, was to render "pure rhythm" visible; pursuing this objective, he had edited non-figurative linear forms and traces of light in sequence on the frames he filmed, so that the organic unity of the images could be perceived, accompanied by music, which could be played during the projection. These were the sort of experiments that would have been shown in the Guggenheim's Ocular Chamber, and they clarify Rebay's ambition in planning its construction. The innovations were to have been an essential component of the life of the museum, which aimed to stimulate the hidden "con-geniality" of each of the museum's visitors with various "geniuses" exposed by the works on display, to paraphrase Alexandre Kojève on the subject of Kandinsky's works.

The request that Wright design this space stemmed from the wish to house and make accessible that which art could produce according to any mode of expression, a path laid open by Kandinsky in his *On the Spiritual in Art*. Here Kandinsky made constant reference to music, its lexicon contributing to the titles of several of his works; it was a useful parallel to explain the contrasts generated by primary colors and demonstrate that what fundamentally separates the painter's work from that of the musician is the possibility the musician has to play with the extension of time. Following this line of thought, but passing over a consideration of its trajectory (particularly in light of the relationship between Kandinsky and Arnold Schönberg, from 1911, the year of both Kandinsky's *On the Spiritual in Art* and Schönberg's *Theory of Harmony*), the Russian painter identified the "basis of concrete art," whose "true enemy is the object," in the "physical affinity" of "vibrations" produced by sound and light. As we read in Kandinsky's "On Stage Composition," in the *Blue Rider Almanac* (1912), the generation of "vibrations" that open the path to "the final goal, (knowledge)," is the "goal of individual means of different arts."

> Guggenheim Museum. Elevation, 1944; section drawing, with detail of the Ocular Chamber to the side, 1944. The auditorium is shown in the basement; the observatory is located at the top of the elevator shaft.

> Guggenheim Museum. Elevation with galleries distributed on hexagonal floors, 1943; study for a design with a hexagonal plan, 1943–44. The galleries are distributed on different floors. At the bottom left, the words "constant ramp" appear in Wright's handwriting.

Rebay generously and ingenuously developed her own, comparable ideas—as the involvement of Fischinger confirms—subject to the influence of Bauer's interpretation. Offering proof of her prodigious optimism, she imagined she could realize them in her "Temple of Non-Objectivity" (which Wright in 1953 provocatively rebuked her for having conceived as the "Bauer House"), and encourage it to flourish thanks to the work of the "wise man" (an epithet she applied to Wright) on whom she had relied. Reiterating that at times the obviousness of ideas holds no significant influence over the originality and beauty of formal invention inspired by them, the architect did not betray the faith placed in him. As can be seen in the initial versions of the project, Wright supported Rebay, to the point of obsequiously proposing to place a crystal observatory, prosaically, at the summit of the elevator shaft—as the hasty sketch which brought the concept to shape demonstrates. Upon reaching the observatory, those who came to the "temple" would be able to enjoy a close-up view of celestial bodies—the most "objective" view the human eye can observe, though Hilla felt it to be one of the sources of inspiration for Kandinsky's "non-objective" paintings. Her interpretation was rather reductive, compared to what Kandinsky maintained in his theoretical writings and repeated also in 1937 during an interview he granted to Karl Nierendorf. On that occasion, Kandinsky had affirmed: "Abstract painting leaves behind the 'skin' of nature, but not its laws . . . cosmic laws. Art can only be great if it relates directly to cosmic laws and is subordinated to them." He specified, however, that "one senses these laws unconsciously if one approaches *nature* not outwardly but—inwardly. One must be able not merely to see nature, but to *experience* it. As you see, this has nothing to do with using 'objects.' Absolutely nothing!"

On considering these passages, it is opportune to return to the project Wright was working on between the end of 1943 and the first months of 1944 and consider its evolution in greater detail. When examining the drawings, one should keep in mind that the choice of the site the designs refer to has only relative importance.

Wright's first scheme, from June 1943, is characterized by the presence of a taller volume, on the right when facing the museum, with a hexagonal floor plan and connected to a vertical, cylindrical block with stairs and elevators that towers above it. A second volume is composed of volumes of different

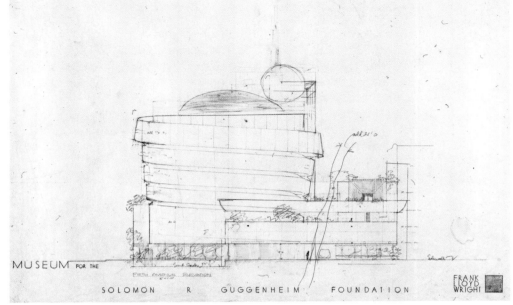

MUSEUM FOR THE

SOLOMON   R   GUGGENHEIM   FOUNDATION

FRANK
LLOYD
WRIGHT

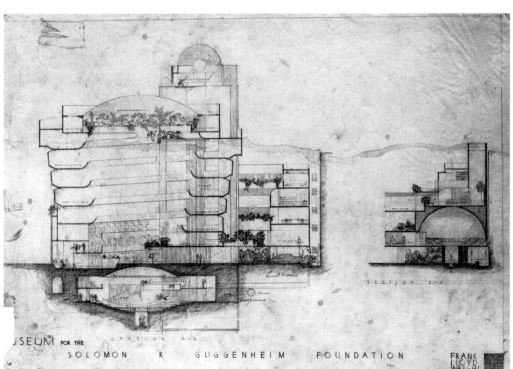

USEUM FOR THE

SOLOMON   R   GUGGENHEIM   FOUNDATION

FRANK
LLOYD
WRIGHT

SCHEME C

THE SOLOMON R GUGGENHEIM FOUNDATION

THE SOLOMON R GUGGENHEIM FOUNDATION — MUSEUM FRANK LLOYD

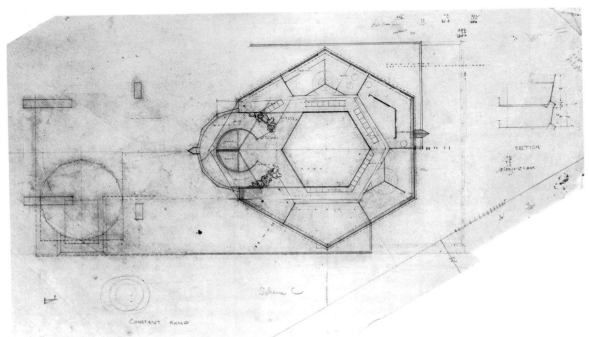

SECTION

Scheme C

CONSTANT RAMP

heights and is joined at 90 degree angles; it rises up from a pedestal used as a terrace but is still formally unresolved. Topped by a geometrically interrupted parapet, this portion of the building protrudes and is suspended on surrounding volumes containing the entrances, which offer access to the facilities planned for the ground floor. The walls of the hexagonal tower, bearing a heavy crown, are divided by five masonry sections and are tilted, opening up like a flower, under continuous skylights. The skylights were to be composed of Pyrex tubes and would allow light to diffuse from above in the galleries, which were not yet designed in spiral form. Here, however, it is important to note that in the floor plan of this version, "scheme C," Wright made an annotation of remarkable importance: a small sketch accompanied by the words "constant ramp." It was thus that the architect communicated to his collaborators that he had decided to join the floors with a rising spiral, whose nature was of course still hypothetical. In light of the subsequent variations of the project, prepared within only a few weeks, this detail demonstrates how Wright, from the end of 1943, was bent on linking the galleries with a continuous spring, and in consequence abandoned the idea of a hexagonal footprint. That this decision matured over the last weeks of 1943 is confirmed by a letter dated January 20, 1944, in which Wright informed Rebay of his intention. In writing to her, he uses incisive phrases and a colorful image, a cryptic crude aphorism explaining the idea that would become the unquestionable guiding line for the project from that point forward: "A museum should be one extended expansive well proportioned floor space from bottom to top—a wheel chair going around and up and down, throughout."

The 1943 plans, drawn when the project was still in an embryonic phase, show the galleries laid out on separate floors, but allow us to observe the originality of the floor plan's structure taking precedence over the formal conception. Accentuated by the pale marble cladding, the emphasis on the horizontal lines of the volumes on the left, separated from the hexagonal prism housing the galleries, evokes compositional and building solutions that Wright had already tested. Among these is one of his most famous works, Fallingwater, at Bear Run, Pennsylvania (1936–38), where, just as in the Johnson Administration Building, for the cantilever base of the structures Wright employed the same collaborators at the museum, including William Wesley Peters. Taken together with the fact that the volumes rising from the platform above the entry, on the left of the view, present banal concepts for the cladding, reprising those adopted in earlier constructions (for example, the Willey and Sturges houses, from the 1930s), we can see why this first version of the museum plans gives but a pallid preview of the most characteristic aspect of the construction visible today. The project evolved rapidly, however, and the volume became a "monolith without joints." "Anything more modern, less stuffy and conventional, you have never seen," Wright declared in a letter sent to Rebay in January 1944. Nevertheless, the compositional strategy, the hierarchy imposed on the masses, and the layout defined in the earliest studies constitute the wellspring for the development of the projects through which, over the next thirteen years, the final design would take shape—the fruit of a progressive and radical reduction of volumes to a seamless accretion.

The successive versions of presentation boards for the project display these choices regarding organization and layout, but differ from the first in that they show the sequence of exhibition rooms with a long, continuous ramp twisting around a void in the center, toward the top. At the start of 1944, having made the decision about the ramp layout—persistent in spite of the long-term polemics it triggered—Wright now seemed to be developing two conceptually similar, but formally opposite, proposals at the same time. During the first months of 1944 he prepared a new project, as the logical precursor to the definitive design, replacing the main structure having a hexagonal floor plan with a tall spiral—in his own words a "ziggurat." In this case, however—exactly the reverse of the famous shape the museum would finally take—the spiral harmoniously narrows as it rises, following the same formal (but not static) principle illustrated by the project for the Gordon Strong Automobile Objective. The ziggurat, thus made the object of a new "consecration," further confirmation of Wright's link between the spiral and an ecumenically accessible form, dominates the whole of the construction, filling the slope on the right-hand side of the presentation drawing, and counterposing the irresolute composition of lower rectangular volumes, in the Monitor, on the opposite side. The project evolved as a montage of selected and schematically defined shapes, raised over an extended and stretched pedestal. It prefigures a construction type prone to producing an unexpectedly captivating sculptural and spatial effect. The entry has the

Guggenheim Museum, entrance on Fifth Avenue, view showing the dilatation of the spiral's base above the "drum" and the entrance to the auditorium

appearance of a deeply dug space excavated at the base of the spiral, in correspondence with the angle of the lot, so that it isolates the first coil of the spring, whose breadth appears to be suspended in the void. It is perhaps a stretch, but we might imagine that this conception was the formal origin from which the highly protruding and circular dilatation derived. Conceived to house the museum's archive, to this day it stands in front of the corner of the construction by 88th Street towering over the ramp that descends toward the auditorium. Still, the formal problem represented by the elevator shaft appears unresolved. Moreover, as in the preceding design, the mostly undefined volume grafted onto the top floor of the edifice, partially overlooking it, prefigures a design that will later be coherently reformulated.

At the same time, adopting marginal variations with regard to the layout, Wright created another version of the project in which he contrasted opposing proposals for the whole structure's color scheme; still he maintained, as he explained to Rebay in 1945, "since I came of age I've never

attributed to any particular color any special Symbolism. . . .
There is no bad color." In this case, though the proposed
cladding was bright and reddish, he aimed for a monochrome
look to harmonize and visually fuse the sections of the building;
and yet, while the spectacular design for the entry, which we
have discussed, was reconfirmed, the ziggurat, on the other
hand, was once again upturned.

Observing them side by side, the boards representing
the project's different configurations seem to have been
designed to astound, given Wright's emphasis on treating the
form like a palindrome. Examining a drawing of the view with
the sectioned spiral, which would lead to the definitive version
of the project (which Wright would work on twelve years later),
a note at the foot of the page calls the inverted spiral a
"taruggiz," the mirror image of a ziggurat.

In contrast with what stands out in the drawings where
the museum has the shape of a ziggurat, in those documenting
the progressive refining of the implication of an upturned
spring—starting from the intuition manifested in the term
"taruggiz," the spirals corresponding to exhibition spaces
appear bigger toward the summit, and grow smaller toward the
bottom, until they join the square base. In this way, too, Wright
shows his intention to provoke an unsettling effect; and further,
because he turns it upside down he makes the spiral a loosely
and freely usable figure and removes all objective, traditional
meanings from it, impressing on the coils a dynamic that
shows clearly how the weight of the structure mounts, in an
unnatural way, as the helix dilates toward the top, increasingly
protruding. The loops of the spiral thus become inscribed in
two upturned cones, of differing heights, whose stability is
ensured by balancing the weights of the protrusions, while its
geometric nature remains highly ambiguous.

While this conception took shape, Wright subjected its
termination to more careful scrutiny. His aim was to make it
suitable to prefigure a blurred assembly of curved shapes in
dialogue with the cylindrical volume of elevators and stairs. At
the same time he progressively lightened the lower support for
the Monitor without attaining a congruous configuration in line
with the conception of the whole building.

Schematic as they were, Wright's designs leave no doubt
that the about-face in the project's shape, on which the whole
composition hinges, was accompanied by the attempt, insis-
tently pursued through the subsequent versions of the project,

ZIGGURAT
ZIKKURAT   TURGEGITZ

Guggenheim Museum. Elevation study
showing a section of the inverted spiral
comprising the main exhibition space.
Sketches to the right show different
versions of the cantilever spring. At the
bottom Wright has written "ZIGGURAT,"
and to the right the palindromic
"TARUGGITZ."

Guggenheim Museum, scheme based on
an inverted spiral. Elevation and section
drawings, 1944

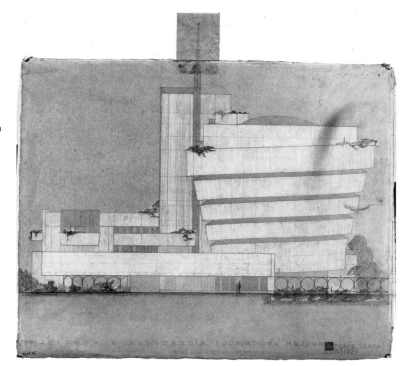

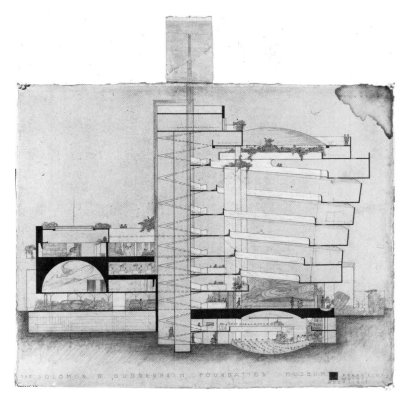

to harmonize the different volumes using continuous bands and lines. Wright expunged any divergences and masked every joint. In this way, the figures he imagined were forced to adapt to the flow of the rising and insistent rhythm of the gallery spirals opening up toward the peak of the building, punctuated by the rhythmic continuity of the protrusions (in contrast to the repeated superposed levels of the Johnson Wax laboratories).

Leaving aside the first version of the project, laid out on a hexagonal floor plan, the watercolor boards prepared between the end of 1943 and the beginning of 1944 set out a series of variations which are exhausted in the "taruggiz" scheme. These express a structural conception, the identification of a cogent building method and formal will, worlds apart from those that had transformed Manhattan, in Wright's opinion, into a "forest of riveted steel posts." Moreover, they show that he aimed to shape a volume that depended on its form alone rather than its traditional and symbolic meaning, one that was indifferent to its location to the point where it could adapt to any situation and setting—the result of a radical interpretation of what his mentor Louis Sullivan had written at the beginning of twentieth century in *Kindergarten Chats*: "A thing looks like what it is, and, vice versa, it is what it looks like."

Several discussions between Rebay and Wright, concerning among other things the color of the building's envelope, accompanied Wright's successive reworking of the designs during the first half of 1945—the year he published *When Democracy Builds*. The book takes another look at the themes behind Broadacre City, the project Mumford reacted to in such a circumspect way that Wright declared to him, "You puzzle me Lewis." The boards prepared in those months were approved and initialed by Solomon Guggenheim, who after putting up feeble resistance agreed to take on the expense of building a model, which Wright urgently advocated, considering the project to be sufficiently developed.

Thus, on September 20, 1945, the model of the Modern Gallery (the name used to refer to the museum between 1945 and 1952) was presented to the public at the Plaza Hotel in New York. The new project had been adapted to the characteristics of the plot of land at Fifth Avenue and 88th to 89th Street, which in the meantime the Guggenheim Foundation had purchased. Despite the lot being narrower and slightly deeper than the one Wright had in mind when making his first designs, the layout of the building did not change much. This configuration Wright

Frank Lloyd Wright, Hilla Rebay, and Solomon Guggenheim in front of the model of the Modern Gallery, New York, August 1945

termed a "logarithmic spiral"—an approximate but effective expression to capture the attention of his patrons and public.

As a continuous floor, it was possible for visitors to walk along the spiral going upward, or take the elevator to the top and walk down. Confusion about the path in which the public would be directed was clarified, with Wright opting for the second choice. Regarding museography, however, Wright stood firmly by his decisions, finding an ally in Guggenheim himself after a visit to Taliesin: the paintings would be displayed in natural light, "freely floated in the sympathetic atmosphere" created around each work thanks to the spatial dilation produced by the wall behind it, tilted and continuous, bounded by the external coils of the spring "which they must accompany."

Concerning its composition, the two main bodies of the construction—that of the galleries and that of the Monitor—are detached from the suspended platform on which they rest. They share the platform only partially, differing in mass and configuration; the Monitor is connected precariously to the upturned spiral, counterposing the latter's dynamic and rhetorically fundamental form with its refined and delicate structure. The Monitor is then capped by the volume holding the apartment intended for the curator, characterized by an excessive aperture onto Fifth Avenue, intended to please Rebay and Guggenheim. The Ocular Chamber is situated at the level below it, with a circular floor plan partially projecting out from the floor supporting it below. The elevator area has a twelve-sided polygonal floor plan, capped by the glass observatory; outside the spiral, it becomes progressively absorbed into the gallery coils, which Wright planned to finish with a sprayed coating of a lightly pigmented plaster, to enhance the cohesive and fluid nature of the form. To tone down the cacophony produced by the bulk of the massive spiral combined with the elevator shaft, and to highlight the shaft's function as a "servant space" (to use Louis Kahn's expression), Wright designed it to be a transparent pillar, clad in Pyrex tubing. To achieve this effect, he turned to a technique similar to the one he had previously tested for the Johnson Administration Building. Moreover, he planned to employ the same material to create the convex roof, a design he would later use in the reception area of the advertising department at the Johnson complex in Racine.

This said, what stands out most in the photographs of the Modern Gallery model, which Wright illustrated to the public on the presentation day, is the way in which the entire

The Modern Gallery. Model, 1945

construction presents itself as a thoroughgoing profession of indivisibility, enjoying its own isolation, protective of its own self-centered freedom. Though, as we have seen, up-ending the spiral of the first ziggurat was palindromic, in examining the model of the Modern Gallery we note how this device has become an essential component of the compositional strategy Wright developed. This version of the project not only reconfigures the spirals of the display areas so that they expand upward before terminating in a heavy circle, it also now plans for the inverted spiral—in preceding plans generally positioned on the right—to be placed on the left, on the 89th Street side. This revolution—reversible in nature as demonstrated by the fact that once it was built the spiral was placed on the opposite corner, at 88th and Fifth Avenue—was not dictated by any serious, functional reason, and is not fully justified by the layout

of the plot. Yet another inversion, involving two out of three planes of the entire construction, this change makes it explicit that the compositional logic guiding the project, since the time it was conceived for an area presumably situated close to fifty blocks away, had the objective of negating, with growing determination, any possibility of comparison and dialogue between the new edifice and the context into which it would have to integrate. For Wright, the land that the museum would occupy was nothing but an available, insignificant bit of blank slate. His sentiment that New York City was not a fertile ground for architecture, seen in his earliest epistolary exchanges with his clients, was thus no improvised paradox. Indeed, as early as 1930, in his lecture "The Tyranny of the Skyscraper," Wright had described all that arises from Manhattan's grid as "a collection of brick and masonry façades,

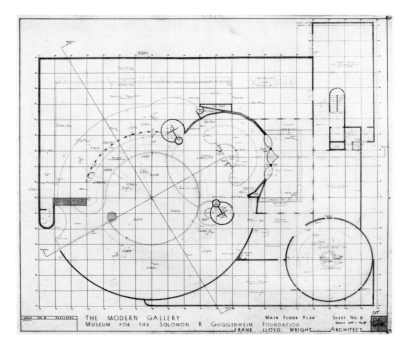

The Modern Gallery, main floor; the Ocular Chamber at the right. Plan drawing, 1945

The Annex. Sketch of the entrance facing 88th Street; plan drawing of the basement, 1947

glaring signs and staring dead walls, peak beside peak, rising from canyons cutting across canyons."

Naturally Wright foresaw the difficulties the project would have to overcome. "Our building is a high speciality which none of the old-line New York firms would (or could) undertake," he wrote to Guggenheim in August 1945, adding that he felt it necessary to aim for a "shortcut" to overcome the more than potential resistance of New York's authorities and agencies. When these obstacles periodically reared up in the subsequent years, along with incidental problems stemming from his patrons' needs when "variations in their circumstances" appeared that "[could] not be covered with the same measure," Wright would always exercise "discretion" and deal with them. In this continuous, flexible, determined work of interpreting situations, Wright's "discretion" might be explained by Aby Warburg's use of the word. Warburg derived its meaning from Francesco Guicciardini (1530) in describing it as deriving from *discernere*, to discern or distinguish, from the Latin *discretus*. This attitude became even more noticeable after the presentation of the model of the museum in 1945, when more precise estimates on the building costs were carried out, considering the construction methods to adopt, how much of the lot to demolish, and the architect's fee on which Wright heavily

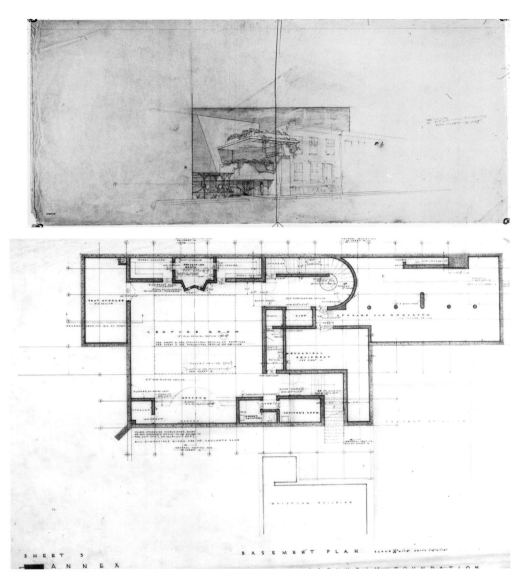

relied to overcome the financial difficulties that constantly plagued him and his practice.

The complexity of these thorny questions and the predictably demanding financial commitments converged, causing a hiatus in the planning during the summer of 1946. This was due in part to Guggenheim's serious concerns regarding economic trends just after the war, but also to disagreements regarding the museum's interior layout roiling the relationship between Wright and

Rebay. Nevertheless, the following year Solomon approved a new project for a small portion of an area previously occupied by a residence and facing onto 88th Street that had been purchased by the Guggenheim Foundation in order to satisfy its needs for more space to accommodate the foundation's own quarters. Wright proposed to build on it a new, modest edifice, called the Annex, that would house services, a conference room, storage, and offices. He aimed to incorporate it into the complex he had already defined. To support this proposal, he modified the Modern Gallery model, the first version of which had gone missing meanwhile. Having done this, he showed that he wanted to configure this narrow and low wing, which he explicitly termed a "buffer" or "bumper," to further isolate the main mass of the museum, interposing a low and elaborate facade in his usual way, between the spiral's anchoring and the screen of buildings on 88th Street. As proof that this was his goal, shortly thereafter he prepared another project for a residential building thirteen floors high; this he designed, however, as a true backdrop to the opposite portion of the lot, toward 89th Street. To accomplish all this, Wright, who was not licensed as an architect in New York, allied himself with Arthur Cort Holden, of the firm Holden, McLaughlin & Associates. Holden would work with him up to the granting of the permit, when he was replaced by another engineer, Jacob Feld, who was more capable of dealing with New York City's Board of Standards and Appeals and was pragmatic in respecting the elements Wright had designed.

These episodes confirm that over the years Wright took every occasion to reiterate his idiosyncratic negation of any type of integration of his work with the built fabric around it, as well as his refusal to have the characteristics of the area condition his choices. It is no coincidence that all the versions of the project, not just the ones we have discussed to this point, fundamentally ignore taking advantage of the proximity to Central Park across Fifth Avenue; the plans systematically excluded any visual continuity between the inward-looking space of the gallery and the expansive background represented by the park, whose appealing scenery can be admired only through limited and partial views. Furthermore, by not changing the spiral configuration when he realized the museum was to be built on Fifth Avenue, Wright offered a striking demonstration of his indifference to the nature of the parcel purchased by the Foundation, commenting on its characteristics using well-mannered terms.

The Modern Gallery. Perspective drawing; in the background, the residential building facing 89th Street, 1951

Guggenheim Museum, skylights on the ramp leading to the auditorium

THE MODERN GALLERY
MUSEUM FOR THE SOLOMON R GUGGENHEIM FOUNDATION
FRANK LLOYD WRIGHT ARCHITECT
HOLDEN · AND · McLAUGHLIN ASSOCIATES

The sketches and especially the renderings that Wright prepared to represent the different evolutions of the project for the Guggenheim are explicit on this matter. The main volume of the museum is nearly always depicted from a low vantage point to emphasize its protruding profile, and it is an understatement to say that little attention is paid to the building fabric around it (and the park), while the Annex on the right and the tall building behind, though their layouts are different, are treated like props for framing the space dominated by the inverted spiral. In contrast, this figure grows outward from the slab, which a deep shadow divides from the ground and whose breadth solemnly reconfigures the parcel's perimeter. It thus offers an abstract, surreal, objectively "non-objective" pedestal for the volumes it towers over (those masses, to this day suspended over the "trench," that defensive trough flanked by the fanciful louvered skylights for the auditorium, and dug out around the point where the spiral meets the ground on Fifth Avenue).

These observations provide an opportunity to critically reconsider one of the most frequent clichés used to explain the peculiarities of Wright's constructions. They were often interpreted as consequent expressions of the empathetic relationship the architect was able to create, holistically and accurately, with the natural places and environs that would host them, "organically" transforming each into a contemporary *locus amoenus*.

Yet it is precisely the construction of the Guggenheim Museum that demonstrates how it is possible to use the expression *genius loci* in Wright's case; provided, however, that the expression is used in its original meaning, as explained by Georges Dumézil in his book *Archaic Roman Religion*, giving the words the meaning that in current usage has been lost. According to Dumézil, *genius loci* is an expression that exposes a state of scarcity, or the appearance of a language's incapacity to name the supernatural being appearing in a specific place. Thus *genius loci* can be associated with the appearance of a condition of separateness and an established border, the exact opposite of the connotation usually attributed to the expression. "Grasp, interpret the *genius loci*, and adapt yourself to it"—these truisms (particularly common in the world of architecture) distort the meaning of an expression that properly alludes to a state of non-participation and apartness, and not to the ancillary function carried out by the characters of places for those who inhabit them. In other words, *genius loci* implies recognition of a condition of outsider-ness, which if we look closely, many of Wright's works express, and which the Guggenheim Museum, more than any of them, illustrates.

Chapter Six
The Angel of the Architects

Wright persevered, carrying on with his drawings and model for the 1945 Modern Gallery and then his 1947 proposals. In defending his designs he showed his obstinacy, equaled by his skill in responding to the observations and objections raised concerning the project, agreeing to modify it without compromising its objectives and design. In 1948, to meet the cost limits established by his patrons, he prepared a series of new modifications reducing the overall dimensions of the building by 380,000 cubic feet. At the same time, however, he placed the spiral close to the corner of Fifth Avenue and 89th Street and maintained the glass dome over the central open space (the project's linchpin, as cross sections dating back to 1944 show). Moreover, in April of that year, after having informed Solomon Guggenheim of the obstacles that would have to be overcome in order to build the museum with a budget of only $2 million, Wright was proposing an extreme alternative. He was equal parts stubborn and indifferent to the implications and characteristics of the area purchased for construction; so he suggested that Guggenheim sell the plot on the privileged and prestigious Fifth Avenue and turn to the public administration of New York City, trusting Robert Moses once again and returning to an idea Wright had put forward in 1943 and that was dear to him. He aimed to extract a sum that would cover the construction of the work as he had imagined it by selecting "a good site in some of the parks or on some boulevard, free," using the profit from the sale "say a million or more," to build the museum.

But Wright's determination to get his project built truly came out in full force after November 3, 1949, the day Guggenheim passed away, realizing Hilla Rebay's fears that his age (and Wright's) would prevent them from seeing the building realized. In the months thereafter, the architect was on the receiving end of confusing letters and notes from Rebay, trying his patience, and the situation was exacerbated by signals indicating that Rebay's position in the Guggenheim Foundation was precarious. Although in February 1950 he wrote to Rebay that "the situation concerning the Museum has

Harry Guggenheim on the right, with Nina Kandinsky and Thom M. Messer, at the opening of *Vasily Kandinsky, 1866–1944: A Retrospective Exhibition*, Guggenheim Museum, January 1963

become too equivocal for me," Wright did not cease to hold his ground, requesting that his prerogatives as a professional be respected. In doing so, he distanced himself from Hilla—though the following passage from a letter he sent to Arthur Holden in February 1950 makes "distancing" seem a euphemism: "Perhaps you don't size up the 'Museum' situation correctly. I am dealing there with an ambitious, ignorant (yes, ignorant of her own thesis) woman whom the Foundation trustees wish to be rid of. I am trying to keep her in because SRG would wish it. But if I ever succeed in building the thoroughbred building I planned for SRG it appears that it will not be because of her but rather in spite of her." Though after Solomon's death the opinions of many of the foundation's trustees favored abandonment of the project, Wright managed to prevent this by gaining the support of his patron's heirs: Eleanor, Solomon's daughter and wife of Arthur Castle-Stuart, from 1950 president of the Guggenheim Foundation, and, especially, of the president of the foundation's board of trustees, Solomon's nephew Harry Guggenheim, and his wife Alicia.

Nevertheless, this tricky phase was another brake slowing the project's development; the reworkings and revisions Wright had to prepare caused laborious negotiations and small diplomatic skirmishes, along with several discussions about the fee he was to expect. Still, on October 4, 1951, Wright informed Albert Thiele, then president of the foundation, that the drawings for the museum were nearly finished and declared he was ready to present them to the foundation's trustees at the end of December. Over the next few months, the project was submitted to the New York City Department of Buildings, which Wright felt he could take on, optimistically trusting in Robert Moses's help and the skill of Arthur Holden. Naturally, Wright did not ignore or underestimate the difficulties inherent in this step; as early as 1945 he had felt it necessary to reassure Rebay, who feared them, explaining to her his pragmatic strategy for overcoming obstacles: "Let me assure you that *our* permit will not be one we will get by standing in line at the City Hall—but a special permit with Moses' help and the good will of the Building Commission."

In March 1952 an updated version of the plans reached Thiele from Taliesin, showing how the passage of years had contributed to giving the museum its definitive configuration. Next, the plans were presented by Holden to the New York officials in charge of granting building permits. While this practice encountered apparently insurmountable obstacles, the situation became even more complicated when the foundation decided to replace Rebay, who had received serious criticism, especially on the part of Aline Louchheim, a New York journalist and future wife of Eero Saarinen. In 1951 Rebay resigned, and one year later James Sweeney was appointed director of the museum; the name was changed shortly after from the Museum of Non-Objective Painting to the Solomon R. Guggenheim Museum, its definitive name.

Hilla accused Wright of being complicit in the foundation's choice and in return received a reply that sheds light on many aspects of their relationship, as well as some twists and turns from the past. "Dear Hilla, what nonsense you wrote," Wright began, brushing off Rebay's complaints, in his letter of December 22, 1953 (which is usefully read alongside the one he wrote to Holden three years prior, cited above). "I have said and say for the record that the form of expression called 'non-objective' is the most advanced form of painting I know. . . . But the term 'non-objective' I do not like because actually the form of expression is the most objective imaginable if the word is to have its proper English meaning. I have said this repeatedly to both you and S.G.H. with no effect. Semantics is not a negligible science. . . . I am standing alone for what SRG employed me to do. I intend to do it, come hell, high water or any interference. Even yours, Hilla."

The letter does not end there, however, and in the subsequent lines Wright brought in the person whose advent

> The Modern Gallery. Perspective, 1951; section, 1952–53; main floor, plan drawings, 1952 and 1953

THE MODERN GALLERY
MEMORIAL MUSEUM FOR THE SOLOMON R GUGGENHEIM FOUNDATION
FRANK LLOYD WRIGHT · ARCHITECT

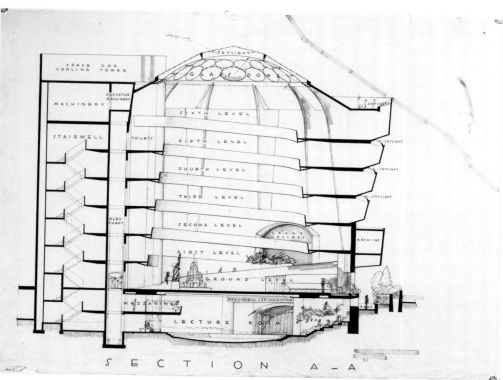

SECTION A-A

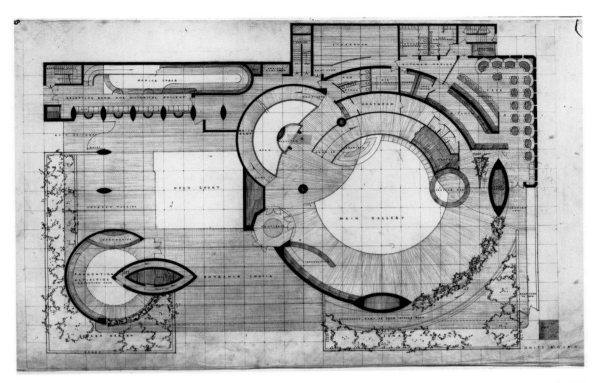

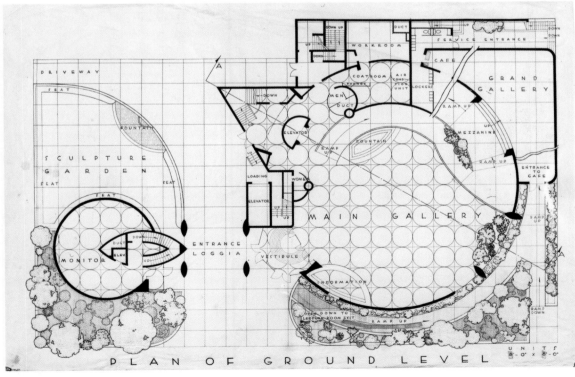

PLAN OF GROUND LEVEL

was at the root of Rebay's protests, James Johnson Sweeney; and from that moment on Sweeney would take center stage in the story. Although he does so hastily, Wright explains to Hilla his opinion of the museum's new director and implicitly reveals the reasons why in the years to come he would clash with Sweeney, ever more bitterly. "Sweeney himself seems to be a regular Museum-man with regular connections." The letter continues with some hunches that would prove to be valid: "I do not know how far he can go—even if he would go—in the direction of not just another museum to exploit a painting, instead of displaying the beauty of paintings in human scale to make them attractive and available to human beings in their natural habit and environment. This I do not yet know and can only hope."

Between 1951 and 1952, Wright's clients' request to respect the ceiling of $2 million for the construction led Wright to rework the project once again. The main modifications concern the height of the spiral—which was reduced—while the curve extended all the way to the ground. This was a consequence of removing the intermediary floor, present in the plans until that point, which was to have been situated between the start of the ramp and the entry point. Moreover, the elevator shaft was partially included in the volume of the spring and, consequently, the plan to use glass tubes as cladding was abandoned; it had become obvious that, following the standards of the New York City building authority, it was preferable to envelop the building in reinforced concrete. Lastly, once the idea of planning an apartment for Rebay in the building was dropped, the Monitor became settled in its configuration, identifiable as a low, cylindrical form; though redundant and still not resolved in its details, it was in harmony with the enveloping bands of the structures below it; inside, this wing had a simplified functional program compared to the one agreed on with Rebay. Nevertheless, what is striking is that this cylindrical figure, counterposed to but functionally connected with the spiral, was served by a very elegant circular stairwell, now occupying the corner of the area framed by Fifth Avenue and 89th Street. This reversal was pivotal in definitively shifting the "taruggiz" to the opposite side of the lot. And this was the parting shot of Wright's plan to create the appearance of objectivity of the meanings evoked by the shapes he used, setting the stage himself to put on a final, virtuoso performance.

Though confrontation with the authorities in charge of granting the building permit carried on heatedly, even inducing

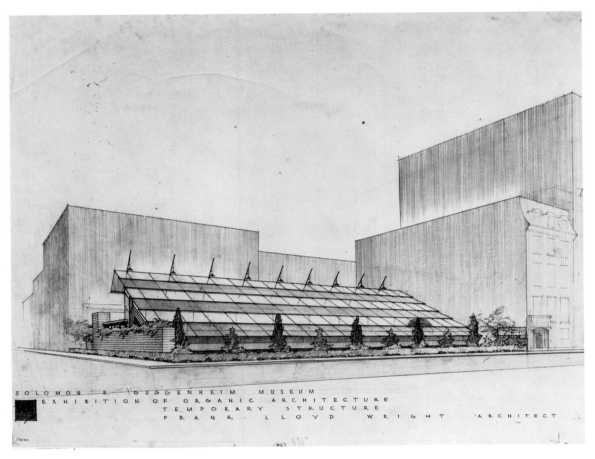

SOLOMON R. GUGGENHEIM MUSEUM
EXHIBITION OF ORGANIC ARCHITECTURE
TEMPORARY STRUCTURE
FRANK LLOYD WRIGHT ARCHITECT

Temporary pavilion for the exhibition *60 Years of Living Architecture*, New York, 1953. Perspective of the pavilion located on the future site of the Guggenheim Museum

Wright to plan a further version of the project at the end of 1953, that same year he constructed a temporary pavilion on the land that the museum would occupy. Sensing the symbolic significance of this, and going against Sweeney's wishes, he insisted on and obtained access to the pavilion through the main entrance of the existing museum. The goal of this construction was to hold the traveling exhibition devoted to his works, *60 Years of Living Architecture*; the exhibition had been presented at Palazzo Strozzi in Florence in 1951, giving Wright the excuse of visiting Florence once more, and Venice. An earlier exhibition devoted to Wright had been held at MoMA in 1940. As a follow-up exhibition had never been realized there, this new international show was a further step in Wright's campaign to woo public opinion. The success it found, also thanks to Wright's position in some of the most influential

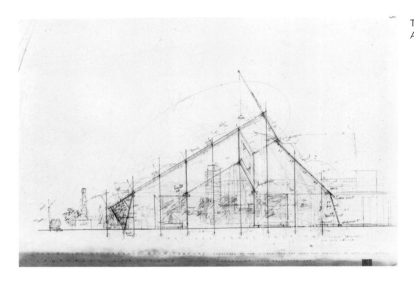

circles in New York, contributed to cementing the decision to build the museum, which by then was all but irreversible. Thus, after having subjected his project to further fine-tuning and adjustments, in March 1956 the Board of Standards and Appeals, approving the architect's application, allowed the Department of Buildings to grant the building permit it had previously refused.

In this very delicate phase, Sweeney's resistance and ill-timed requests produced further delays and complications in the relationship between the architect and his patrons. These were so worrying that on March 9, 1956, only a few weeks before construction work started, Wright addressed the museum's director thus: "Dear James, Since you became the Guggenheim curator I have wondered why you never asked me what best use you could make of the idea of the museum as it existed. Then when the new plans were made you were taken in and so far as I know all your suggestions were adapted at an extra cost of several hundred thousand dollars. Now, at the final moment without warning you go back on the whole thing and show by your demands that you have never really taken in the idea of the museum as planned. . . . Now one of two things—either you do not know this because you do not appreciate the building or, as gossip has had it, you tend to prevent its erection."

Clearly, Wright was aware that these were not simply rumors; exactly two days before he sent this letter, he wrote to Harry Guggenheim advising him to dismiss not only Sweeney but also his wife, Laura, whom he considered an adversary as dangerous as her husband: "Laura for some reason or none, is poison to the Guggenheim family. I hate to think of her in Uncle Sol's memorial. Have you ever thought of young Edgar Kaufmann of the Museum of Modern Art for the driver seat? Not too young in the ways of artists, Edgar is more erudite, honorable and sensitive than Jim." This last suggestion is typical and sheds light on how Wright—after being in conflict with Rebay for years, clashing with Sweeney, and aware of his advancing age—felt such a compelling necessity, just before the construction started, to be able to count on a reliable associate at the head of the museum that he gave Harry Guggenheim such biased advice as to appear ingenuous. By 1956 Edgar Kaufmann was no longer head of the Industrial Design Department at MoMA, contrary to what Wright seems to have believed; there were certain ties binding them— Kaufmann had joined the Taliesin Fellowship as an apprentice in 1934, and moreover he was the heir to the fortune of the Kaufmann family that had commissioned fourteen projects from Wright, of which three were built, including Fallingwater.

It is therefore no surprise that in the following months the relations between Wright and the museum director became even more strained, subject to various conjectures and biased interpretations. An apparently eccentric witness sheds further light on this relationship, in a brusque and efficient way; the episode moreover explains the list of names Moholy-Nagy gave to Rebay in 1943, discussed earlier, at the time when Rebay was looking for an architect to whom the museum project could be entrusted. Four months before Wright's death, and ten months before the museum opened, Louis Carré sent a letter to his architect friend Alvar Aalto that gives us a view into the situation at that time. Carré was a French collector and art dealer who had organized an exhibition in 1935 titled *Les arts primitifs dans la maison d'aujourd'hui* in Le Corbusier's apartment building in Rue Nungesser-et-Coli in Paris, where he lived as well, and in 1956 he had commissioned Aalto to design a house at Bazoches-sur-Guyonne. In the 1950s Carré regularly went to New York and would write from there to Aalto, sending him news on events he felt would interest the Finnish architect. His letter of December 3, 1958, contains information that allows us to intuit the atmosphere in artistic circles and in New York's bon ton around the imminent opening of the new Guggenheim building. Moreover, Carré's words as a

Frank Lloyd Wright and George N. Cohen at the Guggenheim Museum construction site, 1958

Epigraph at the entrance of the Guggenheim Museum

disinterested observer depict how much the relationship between Sweeney and Wright had deteriorated over the five years since 1953—when Wright had spoken to Rebay about the new director, calling him "a regular Museum-man." Carré wrote to Aalto: "A few weeks ago, the plan was to move into the new Museum at the start of January, but now I hear that there is a further delay of five or six months. Thus, it seems things are not going very well, and some say that Sweeney wished Wright would die before construction began in order to be released from the contract. However, he does not know that there is a special angel that protects the great architects."

This angel had already shown it was capable of watching over the architect under its care. Construction work for the building of the Guggenheim Museum had begun two years earlier—August 16, 1956, to be exact. Wright lived in his suite at the Plaza Hotel, while the construction, to which we will now turn our attention, was directed by William Short of the firm Holden, McLaughlin & Associates, and the contractor George N. Cohen, whose name is to this day duly remembered alongside that of Wright in the inscription at the museum's entrance.

Chapter Seven
A Building to Withstand the Atomic Bomb

In 1945, illustrating the model of the Modern Gallery and explaining the characteristics of the construction of the coil he had designed and what the structure would provide, Wright astonished the audience gathered in New York for the presentation. On that occasion he made use of a disconcerting image, promptly recorded by the press, and related also by *Architectural Forum* to its readers in January 1946. After having explained that the building's form was "a true logarithmic spiral" made up of a single element, from bottom to top, joined to the external cladding and the internal parapet, Wright shocked the crowd by declaring: "When the first atomic bomb lands on New York [the building] will not be destroyed. It may be blown a few miles up into the air, but when it comes down it will bounce!" In December 1959, eight months after Wright's death, Lewis Mumford recalled this jolting and unnerving remark in his article in the *New Yorker* on the Guggenheim, which had finally opened to the public. Though it was the result of debatable considerations, the conclusion in a central passage in this brief essay contained a section that once again looked at the relationship between Wright and New York which is useful to relay. "Wright was a master of texture, in brickwork not less than in stone. Yet in this building, by its nature a show-piece, he was content to emphasize the sheer elephantine solidity of heavy concrete walls," wrote Mumford. After having openly shown that he had misunderstood the conception of the Guggenheim from the highly debatable point of view that had led him to call Wright "a master of texture," Mumford followed with the acerbic words: "Did he design the Guggenheim Museum as a super-pillbox that would resist vandalism or demolition as effectively as those surviving concrete bunkers Hitler's minions built along the Channel coast? Wright is reported to have said that if a nuclear bomb destroyed New York, his building would merely bounce with the shock and survive. Thus Wright would be left, in effect, surveying the ruins, ironically triumphing over the city that had waited till the end of his life to give him this one opportunity."

Having come to this point, we will not pursue the matter further; this is not the place to explore the complex and ambiguous relations between Mumford and Wright over the course of their lives, as reflected in their invaluable epistolary exchanges. Rather, it would be timely to ask to what extent this staggering image the architect evoked in 1945 guided the way in which the museum was actually built.

Comparing the edifice to a spring capable of bouncing off the ground, Wright intended to show that the museum's spiral corresponded to the weight-bearing structure and form of the construction. As we have seen, it was a theme that Wright had worked on for decades. Solomon Guggenheim and Hilla Rebay gave him the opportunity to develop it and bring it to extreme conclusions. However, the "museum" Hilla had been imagining had various precedents that she did not neglect to mention when speaking to Wright about linking rooms, floors not connected by stairs, and flowing spaces adapted to house the masterpieces of non-objective painting that she had collected. In a strange coincidence, however, the friend of hers who had planted the idea of "endless spaces," Frederick Kiesler, would not become her architect, as Kiesler was chosen by Peggy Guggenheim for her museum, precluding to Hilla a choice that otherwise would have been natural. Nevertheless, the "tension skyscraper" (1925), the Space Theatre for Woodstock, New York (1931), the *Raumbühne* displayed in Vienna with Léger (1924), and other works by Kiesler prepared before he designed Art of This Century were not the only examples Rebay may have been pondering, as already suggested, when working with Wright toward making the Guggenheim project satisfactorily meet her aspirations.

Among these examples there is one that deserves special attention. In June 1939, Hilla was in London with Solomon. There they likely met with Le Corbusier, who showed them a project for a "musée d'Art moderne (en spirale carrée), à croissance illimitée"—a modern art museum (in a rectilinear spiral shape) of unlimited growth. The design was translated into "two superb models that [would] be displayed [t]here the following week." Le Corbusier spoke of the project in a letter to his mother, excerpts of which figure here, sent from London on June 3, 1939. The project was the development of the Musée Mondial, a design within the Mundaneum scheme that he had

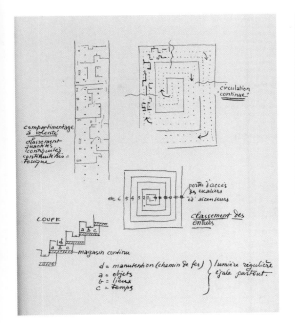

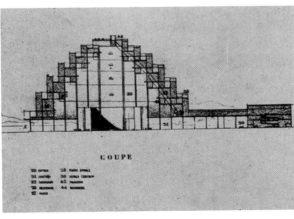

Le Corbusier, Mundaneum, Musée
Mondial, 1929. Overview sketches;
section

worked on in 1929. It had an "organic form," which "is a triple
nave unfolding along a spiral." Le Corbusier confidently presented the models of the Musée à croissance illimitée in June
1939, which were soon to be exhibited in Paris, and in London
as well they were destined to come to the attention—"with a
good possibility of future opportunities," Le Corbusier confided
to his mother—of an exceptional personage: "Guggenheim,
copper king of New York." As we know, there would be no
"possibility of future opportunities" for Le Corbusier's project.
And this episode remains a sort of mystery—if two gossamer
threads, so difficult to unravel but nonetheless illuminating, a
surprise that history reserves for those who turn their attention
to it, had not come to our attention. In 1946, around seven years
after Hilla and Solomon likely saw the model of the "musée
d'Art moderne (en spirale carrée)," Kiesler published an article
in the *Partisan Review*, to which Joseph Siry attracted our
attention. On that occasion, Kiesler, who as we know was in the
position to do so, explained how architecture had come to face
the figure of the spiral, and he compared his projects, well
known to Rebay, to Tatlin's design for the Monument to the
Third International, Wright's Modern Gallery, and Le
Corbusier's Musée Mondial. The London encounter with Le
Corbusier and Kiesler's article fuel conjectures about the

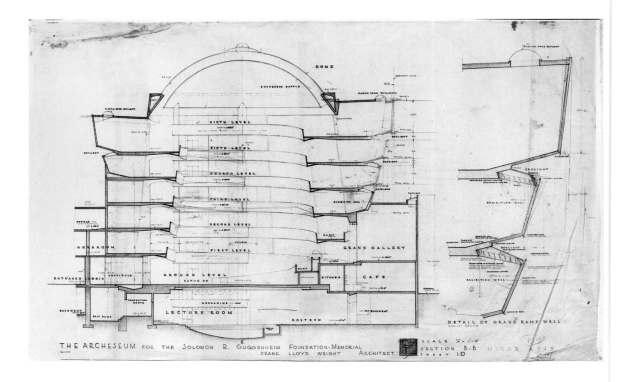

Guggenheim Museum. Section drawing of the version of the project that Wright called "The Archeseum," with detail of the ramp's exterior walls on the fourth, fifth, and sixth levels, 1956

models and options Rebay may have been considering in entrusting the Guggenheim Museum project to Wright, but they do not shed light on a further enigma concerning the project's genesis. In 1994, once restoration works on the museum were finished, the Guggenheim Foundation published a book containing a well-sourced essay by Bruce Brooks Pfeiffer dedicated to the history of the building. In this essay Pfeiffer cites a passage in a letter Wright sent to the client for whom, some years earlier, he had designed the Sugarloaf Mountain complex in Maryland, Gordon Strong. With this letter, which bears the date July 10, 1929, the same year in which Le Corbusier presented his project for the Mundaneum, Wright asked Strong to return to him the drawings of the unbuilt project since, he asserted, "it seems something of the kind is contemplated on the other side, in France, only in that case, it is a museum. Some interest has arisen in this idea as I have worked it out for you and I have been asked many times to see it." According to Pfeiffer, this letter proves that "in 1929 Wright was considering the use of the spiral for an art museum." In reality, Wright's request allows us to think that

A Building to Withstand the Atomic Bomb

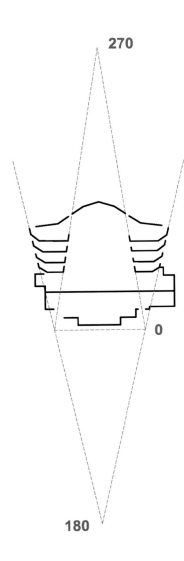

270

0

180

The Archeseum, section corresponding to the minor axis, 1956. The red lines emphasize the interior and the exterior surfaces of the ramps. A three-dimensional representation would show these inverted triangles as cones.

what Pfeiffer considers a demonstration is really only a hypothesis—as plausible as it may be—that should be placed in the context of the common research carried out in nineteenth-century architectural circles on spiral figures. In any case, even if Wright knew of the Mundaneum plans, or conversely if Le Corbusier knew of the project for Strong, that does not lead beyond the observation that there is a conceptual affinity between the projects for the Guggenheim and for the Musée Mondial, even if this conclusion is less than satisfying.

When he had presented the Musée à croissance illimitée, Le Corbusier said that he was convinced of having achieved, after ten years of study, "a substantial result: total standardization of the construction components: a pole, a beam, a ceiling unit." The Modern Gallery, in contrast, substituted a coil for the components of a trilithon structure, with the spiral taking the place of a continuous beam. Furthermore, Le Corbusier's spiral, inscribed in a golden rectangle, is logarithmic; although Wright at times referred to the spiral of the Modern Gallery as logarithmic, it is in fact Archimedean, or arithmetic—a difference the significance of which Hilla could only partially grasp. But once this curious event has been noted, it remains to observe that the spring, which to this day wraps around the inside of the Guggenheim and determines its outside appearance, implies that one was shaped by the other on the basis of a construction decision that had nothing to do with Rebay, and was unrelated to the designs of Le Corbusier or Kiesler.

In the Guggenheim Museum's space, the internal circles rise upward, following a movement dictated by the progressive reduction of the radius; on the outside it is the inverse, and the bands grow larger toward the top, as the diameter increases. "The relationship between these constantly changing radii and the gradually rising plane of the ramp is so arranged," explained the project's contractor, George Cohen, in 1958, "that at any point in the height of the structure a horizontal plane will always intersect a true circle." The building's shape is thus the result of a heterodox geometrical reversal—that is, two virtual cones interpenetrating. Following the inverted protrusions, the cone, which ideally conjoins the points of the external surfaces, has its vertex at 180 feet below ground level, while the vertex of the one joined to the internal ramp is about 270 feet above the ground.

This conception, which aims to guarantee the unity of the shapes through the inversion (in the manner of Hokusai) of

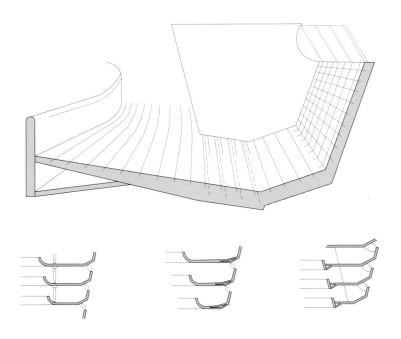

The ramp as a U-shaped beam.
Interpretive drawing

Various solutions explored for the ramp
of the museum: with pillars; with struts
positioned through the openings for the
skylights; with sails, as ultimately built.
Interpretive drawing

the very same geometric figures that shape the space and the
shell, was fine-tuned definitively when the piano nobile was
eliminated, and the continuous ramp was redesigned and set
to start at the ground floor. The coil curving into a tormented
inversion where it intercepts the towers of the elevators and
facilities, still visible to this day, was initially conceived to serve
as the sole helicoid cantilever, without expansion joints, with a
vaguely U-shaped section. The internal edges, around three
feet high, were originally planned to be bent at a nearly right
angle. Without the continuity, the floor with the ramp would
have had to cause, on the side opposite the spiral, a second
inclined contour to allow the external bands to be taller and
broader, separated from each other by narrow, continuous slits
for the skylights. A circular structure in bronze, placed over the
crown above the last and tallest coil would have allowed for
glass tubing to be used in finishing the low dome over the
central void. These proposals were only partially realized, but
they confirm that the project included plans from the beginning
to build the edifice as a single object, like a continuous hull,
resembling a thick and rigid curling skin, and exploiting the
protrusions and features to the hilt. This spiral would

Sketch of the spring's exterior walls with openings for the skylights, c. 1945

Study of the spring's volutes on the fourth, fifth, and sixth levels, c. 1945

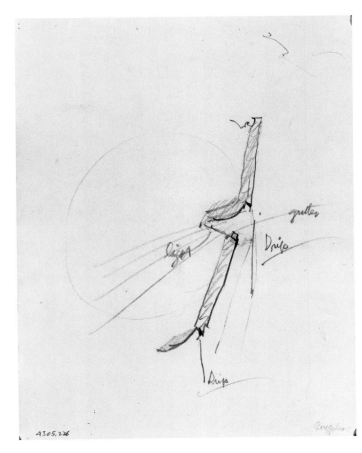

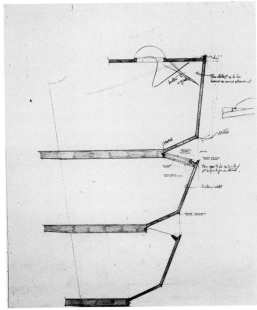

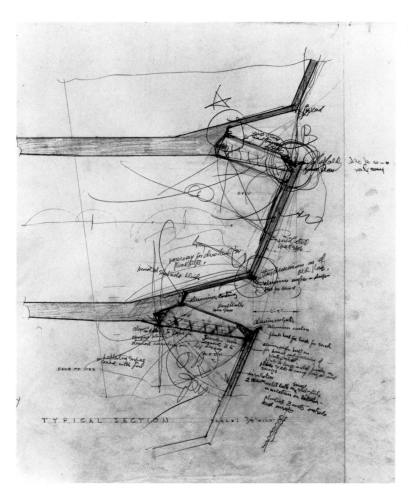

accompany the movement of a helicoid beam, with a lesser pull compared with those that are exerted on flat, circular beams.

A similar notion, the antithesis of a post-and-beam structure, was difficult to reconcile with the culture and mentality prevalent among engineers in New York—as Wright polemically stated. Moreover, it meant that the techniques adopted were in conflict with the habits of the construction companies, the skills of the labor force, the union rules, the building regulations, and the financial means provided by the clients.

Thus, when in August 1956 the work site was launched, a true tour de force began, which forced the builders to use different and not fully congruous techniques, as Stan Allen has

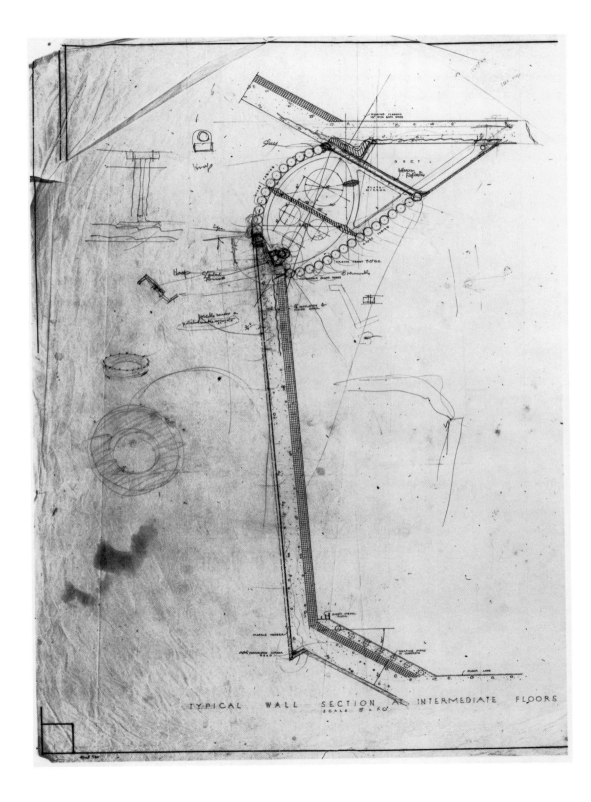

TYPICAL WALL SECTION AT INTERMEDIATE FLOORS

demonstrated. Once the first stone of this building was laid, under the direction of tried-and-true colleagues of Wright such as Mendel Glickman and William Wesley Peters, the work site was managed by Charles W. Spero and William Short, who were in charge of its progress. George N. Cohen, as owner of the modest-sized Euclid Contracting Corporation which had accepted the conditions dictated by the architect and took the contract of building the museum, bore the responsibility for executing the works.

Given the structural conception of the edifice, the principal engineering difficulties to be faced were in the configuration of the cement spiral strip. The spring, similar in function to a continuous beam, with a neutral axis that was no longer arranged as allowed by a beam with a U-shaped section, had a dual curve, rising at an incline of 3 percent, and making

The Guggenheim Museum under construction, c. 1958. View from Fifth Avenue, and view of the corner of Fifth Avenue and 88th Street

six full turns as the diameter of the internal circles decreased toward the top. Imagining the beam as a long, unrolled band with bent edges, the first possibility examined was to insert between the coils a series of pillars, and in the skylight slits place slanted struts. Subsequently, in order to eliminate the vertical supports that would have compromised the spatial continuity of the spiral, a second structural variant was studied, which would have reinforced and bolstered the struts in the

A Building to Withstand the Atomic Bomb

A grid used to draw the loops of the spiral in plan

windows, now positioned at intervals of about 6.5 feet. In order to prevent the negative effects of the weight of the pillars and struts to support the hefty loads and significant tensions, which would have been considerable, and to respect the standards for fire safety, Wright and the engineers devised the structural design they would finally implement, avoiding giving the external bands and the internal parapets a load-bearing function. As can be observed from within the museum, the measures adopted involved constructing twelve inverted triangular ribs, one of which is only partially visible because its end, which the dome rests on, emerges from the column holding the services and the emergency staircase. These ribs are laid out radially, with the pointed vertex joined, at intervals of 30 degrees, to the supporting cylinder, and protruding sharply at the summit. Invisible from the ground floor, with their contours outlined by an acute angle, they emerge at the level of the first coil and then rise up, protruding, toward the roof. With a basic and elegant solution, the two rib vaults inserted beside the stairwell frame the trapezoid-shaped mouth of the stairs.

The purpose of these triangular "sails" has been the subject of various interpretations—the builders referred to them in curiously vague terms, and the beam itself carried different names. In the past, scholars including William H.

Jordy and myself supported the hypothesis that the ribs did not have a structural function in guaranteeing the stability of the helicoid beam, since their purpose was principally to separate the rings of the spring whose weight is borne by the anchoring service shafts. This thesis has now been convincingly refuted by structural engineer Tomaso Trombetti. Having excluded the possibility that the external bands, given their structure, could support the traction forces that the original hypothesis would involve, Trombetti came to the conclusion that the ramp cannot be a continuous, cantilevered helicoid beam because it would have required the use of an armature formed of steel bars with transversal areas that were not foreseen when the museum was being built. Trombetti then observed that the spiral is surrounded at its base by a massive cylinder, and this serves as a support for triangular ribs, reasoning therefore that they support the portion above the third level of the spiral. Since the beam varies in breadth, the section with a constant height (13 inches) therefore rests on the ribs, while the thinner part, holding up the interior parapet, juts out. This thesis is corroborated by a stress analysis and the characteristics of the materials used—including the builders' note specifying 3500 psi concrete, with a slump of between three and four inches, and analysis of the armature; it does not, however, explain the behavior of the deformations. Still, accepting this explanation, the spiral appears to be composed of two distinct parts: for 270 degrees it is a helicoid beam, and for 90 degrees, in the section corresponding to the elevator shafts and stairwell, it is a simple beam on fixed supports.

George Cohen himself noted: "The structural design features rigid slabs with spans up to 60 feet and cantilevers up to 25 feet, some with highly concentrated end loadings. The main ramp cantilevers 14 feet 6 inches to the inner court from a 13 inch deep rigid exterior beam of varying widths. Since the greater widths occur at the higher levels, the overall width of the ramp increases as it spirals upward." Using this explanation as further support, Trombetti concluded that "from an analysis aimed at evaluating the vertical load exerted on the ribs, it emerges how this resultant force is placed at each level nearly on the same vertical axis." For these reasons, joining the spiral to the columns produces continuous movement punctuated by the inversions of the curves in the beam (and the joints are subjected to expansions and dilations, the effects of which are visible, though the instruments used to counteract them are

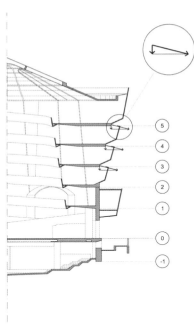

not). The vertical structures and the spring follow their own geometrical logic, as can be seen in the way the curve of the ramp gradually dominates the vertical line of the services tower on the right, exposed at the ground floor, without undergoing any change or deformation. Moreover, the rings of the spring as it joins the vertical pillars nullify any impression of symmetry and react purely to the force, announced by the slight protrusion of the ramp at ground level connecting to the entry of the High Gallery, which fuses and absorbs the different forms of the structural components. The spatial configuration thus stems from a refined balancing of the volumes, and this renders visible the effect of the static conception of the whole construction. Balance is achieved through the progressive protrusion of the ramp in relation to the "two separate corners which the rib vaults form with the vertical axis," Trombetti

Guggenheim Museum, view of the interior from the ground floor

Each ramp discharges its vertical load onto that below in a discontinuous way, through struts that in turn "transfer" the vertical loads to the external bands. Interpretive drawing (T. Trombetti)

The ramp of the Guggenheim is subdivided into twelve sectors, each with a 30 degree angle at the center. Nine sectors, for an extension of 270 degrees, form the actual ramp, a helicoidal beam, while the remaining three sectors, equal to 90 degrees in plan and comprising the stairwells and the elevator shaft, are similar to a traditional post-and-beam structural typology. Interpretive drawing (T. Trombetti)

Between the ground and the third level, the helicoidal beam is surrounded by a cylindrical "drum" functioning as a vertical support for the ramp. The vaulting has a vertical support function for the ramp only at the third level and above. Interpretive drawing (T. Trombetti)

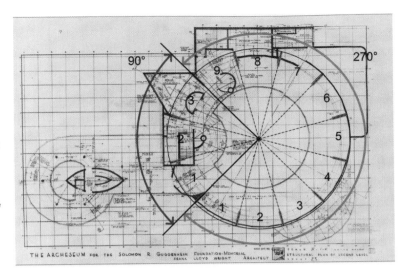

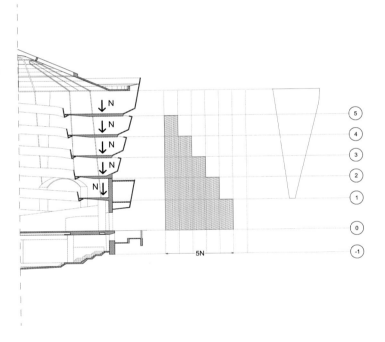

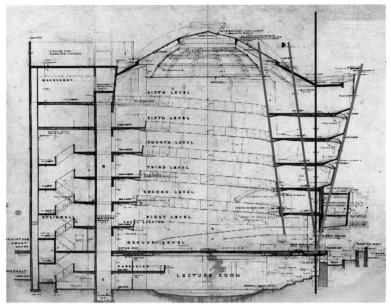

The optimum balance of loads is achieved through the outward projection of the band as it rises, countering the inward projection of the cantilevered ramp. This precise balance explains the existence of two different angles formed at the sides of the vaults against the vertical. Interpretive drawing (T. Trombetti)

Guggenheim Museum under construction, November 1957

notes, around 11 degrees toward the inside and double that toward the outside, and from the decrease in the protruding coil's incline as it goes upward, and thus in its weight.

The methods of construction of the encircling "beam" also underwent a significant evolution, regarding which it is useful to delve into the efforts that were expended to preserve its monolithic character, not only in terms of the form; Jordy has paid particular attention to the latter. The initial calculations took into account a ramp built of reinforced concrete, using a folded, continuous steel net, and a precast-steel structure. Once it was established that this process was not feasible, given the New York City building regulations, the decision to insert the rib vaults above the load-bearing cylinder involved the adoption of a less elegant but simpler building technique: a traditional armature was embedded in the spiral's protruding floor (doubled at the edge to hold a tunnel with a triangular section for the air conditioning), while the steel net, reinforced with horizontal and vertical bars, was used only for the construction of the external bands and the internal parapets, whose weight rests on the spring. In this way, the apparently U-shaped "beam," though lacking joints and being fairly rigid thanks to welding work on the steels bars (work which, as

it happens, was not adequately recorded), is not coherently monolithic, and two different construction methods were employed in producing it. The ramp was formed using tradi- tional cast cement (so not continuous) with light aggregate concrete on a heavy armature, while the exterior bands were molded by spraying cement from the inside onto the steel net, reaching a thickness of around five inches, employing form- work only on the outside in order to reduce costs and limit the need for expensive scaffolding. For the interior parapets and railings, however, traditional cement was used. Siry has so thoroughly described both the building process and techniques used in this regard that we recommend all who wish to delve further into this aspect of the building history to refer to his writings, as we will touch on it only briefly. In particular, Siry has reconstructed the process which led Wright to use gunite, a mixture of cement, light aggregate, and water that is sprayed through a pressure hose; for the Guggenheim's construction, the main advantages were reducing weight and facilitating the production of curved surfaces. This choice, which turned out to be essential to obtaining the shape and balance sought, and was also pivotal in establishing the building's intrinsic fragility and perishability, was no impromptu decision. As Siry has demonstrated, Wright had for some time contemplated and tested gunite, well before 1956. He was influenced both by Richard Neutra's experience in building the Lovell House in Los Angeles (1927–29) as well as, very probably, by what Wright knew about Le Corbusier's trials of this building technology. Back in 1923, Le Corbusier had suggested to his client Henri Frugès that the cement gun technique be implemented, using equipment produced in the United States and publicized in *L'Esprit Nouveau*, in the construction of the small housing complex in Lège and of the Quartier Moderne in Pessac; putting it into practice, however, he obtained rather disappointing results as regards the construction. (For the Guggenheim, however, while gunite achieved remarkable results in terms of load distribution and facilitating construction and form, it was not sufficient to ensure the work's durability.) Use of the material reduced the weight of the exterior bands resting on the continuous beam within and made it

considerably easier to move the formworks and reduce their expansion, molding the coil like a smooth ribbon. Gunite not only resolved the problems posed by formworks, allowing them to be efficiently reused, making their construction and the priming of the provisional works easier, but it also made it possible to avoid, once the works were already underway, a compromise Wright had earlier proposed. That compromise was presented by Wright in 1956, as work at the site was just beginning. In the boards he submitted, he called this proposal "The Archeseum," and in the drawings the plan and consequently the shell were given a polygonal configuration. That design would have rendered the carpentry work easier and allowed for expansion joints to be placed—an issue of investigation not wholly resolved even after the restoration work on the museum between 2004 and 2008 was carried out. However, the polygonal design was set aside when, as the works proceeded, Wright felt it was not necessary to make this compromise. Nevertheless, the continuity of the surfaces and the gyrating effect of the ramp's movement, which make the Guggenheim unique, were the result of ceaseless adjustments and well-camouflaged compromises. Two key resolutions had to be met to achieve this effect. The first led to the sacrifice of the exterior cladding; beginning in 1944, this became the object of various studies, as well as conflicts and debates, and later of cost evaluations. The exterior was simply tinted with a glazing that softened, but did not mask, the rough imperfections resulting from the unavoidable work of refinishing the malleable materials. And yet, it is thanks to this sacrifice, another element imposed by the passing of time, that the rough surfaces—within and without—enhance the chiaroscuro effects and make visible the unequalled, intimate coherence of the building. This coherence is the fruit and the manifestation of the work of molding that takes advantage both of the malleability of the material making up the building's structure and the shaping of space with the convexities and concavities of the bodies that structure it. It is the result not of the overlaying and intersection of the floors, but rather of the fluid composition of a sequence of points of tension, lacking facets, plastic and not sculptural—at its heart the museum's form thus possesses a tactile eloquence. It was the century in which architecture coincided with the advent of what Ernst Bloch called the "sovereign reign of washability," and the Guggenheim is an apt expression of this condition. Ennobled by its shape built with

Guggenheim Museum, interior and exterior views

the lowliest materials, the incessant curves of the edifice make its harmony tangible—a harmony that is in reality made up of numbers and geometric figures, the richest materials an architect can rely on.

The second decision, no less challenging, involved the roof over the central space; as work progressed, a solution developed that was radically different from the one originally planned. After acknowledging that it would be impossible to re-create in the museum what he had tested out in his building for Herbert Johnson in Racine, at first Wright thought he could resolve the matter of the cupola by inserting transparent surfaces in a lacunar structure. Discarding this option as well, he proceeded to design what was eventually built, a compromise solution that could be created relatively quickly, thus resolving the dangerous consequences he was facing by the strictures of time.

As those who visit the museum can observe, on top of the twelve ribs, positioned like the hours on the face of a clock, are six prefabricated beams, inclined and protruding, in the shape of hairpins, or open upside-down U-shapes, very elongated and thin. Used in this illusory and ambiguous cupola they evoke stability, serving as meridians joined by six cement segments, like horizontal struts, situated below the apexes of the curves. Working in tandem with these summits, the struts form a heterodox keystone, or a circle that finishes off the dome, where the parallel lines converge without imposing monolithic continuity. This system only partially rests on the extrados of the ribs; the beams do not entirely weigh on them; they do, however, exert a force on their lateral contours and in this way help to stabilize them, working by compression, to reinforce the eminently empirical character of the building's final stability. The reduction of glass surfaces thanks to the insertion of an inclined cement diaphragm, which extends from the cover of the last ring and bending upwards offers the structure a taut band, makes it more difficult still to perceive the static ambiguity of the dome. This feature contributes to the blending, visually at least, of the break in the structural continuity, thus resolving the form in a pragmatic way of one of the most critical passages, in the configuration of the internal, private space of the spectacularly light and translucent roof that Wright had originally imagined.

And yet it is precisely the ways in which the structural problems were dealt with, and the coherent and creative

The Archeseum. Design for the glass roof of the cupola, c. 1956

The glass roof of the cupola as built is supported by U-shaped beams, "hairpins," protruding out of the sixth level. The connecting elements join the "hairpins" as concentric rings. Interpretive drawing (T. Trombetti)

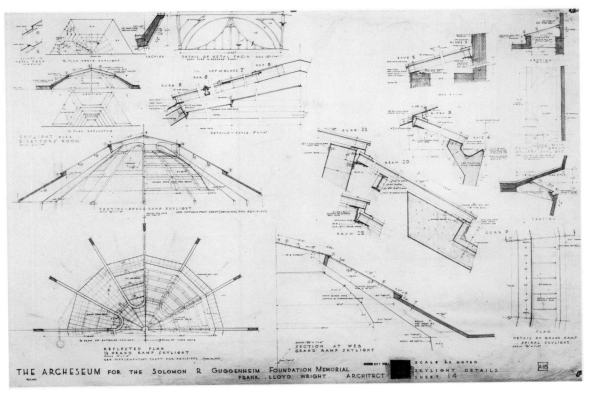

THE ARCHESEUM FOR THE SOLOMON R GUGGENHEIM FOUNDATION MEMORIAL
FRANK LLOYD WRIGHT ARCHITECT

SCALE AS NOTED
SKYLIGHT DETAILS
SHEET 14

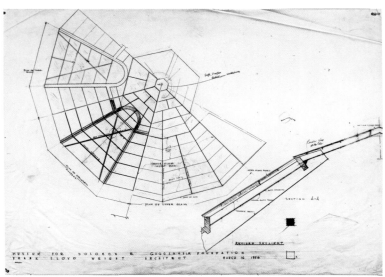

Drawing of the structure of the glass roof of the cupola, 1958

Glass roof of the cupola under construction, 1958

Glass roof of the cupola

empiricism of the solutions adopted during construction, that demonstrate how at the museum work site the results of a complicated tangled jumble of adjustments were skillfully and successfully spun together. Availing himself of a warp, "what reality wants from the work," and a weft, "what the artist wants from his work," in Pavel Florenskij's terms, Wright wove a cloth that in the end took on the appearance of a monument. It speaks to the price paid by will in dominating necessity, and stands witness to its success.

Despite the obstacles to overcome in order to realize it, and despite its complexity, the structure reinforces the message that the Guggenheim was intended to communicate. As we have seen, the spring-shaped galleries and the cylindrical Monitor rise from a podium that separates them from the ground, removing them from the "rule of the grid" and freeing them from the net in which Manhattan's city layout captures each and every building, transforming it, Wright was thinking, into a part of a "picturesque" backdrop.

This said, a close examination of the ways in which the museum was built offers further clues, useful especially in bringing into focus the implications of the disconcerting decision Wright made when he upturned the gallery volume and inverted its name. The considerations which have been presented suggest that it would be reductive to view the palindrome that settles once ziggurat takes on the form of "taruggiz" solely as the result of a play on words carried out to demonstrate that free will is the only explanation for the choices made by an architect. Once he decided on this inversion, Wright made the controversial choice to hide the spiral's end, taking the building out of the homogeneous, cinematic rise that Manhattan prosaically imposes on the edifices it hosts.

Upon entering the museum, one can note how the lowest part of the spiral is conceived as the last step of a labyrinthine staircase. There it consumes itself in the ground, at a pool of water in that mandorla shape Wright cherished. Crudely shaped, a vestige of a furnishing intended for the ground floor and explored in various versions, but fated to shrink until it lost itself in its outline, this fountain evokes a center and a termination where all tensions fuse. Using the analogies with which Ananda K. Coomaraswamy explained the symbolism of the dome, this coincides with the point where the arrow launched from the taut cord of the bow, a depiction of the transversal section of any domed building, crosses the eye.

But at the Guggenheim, the eye does not draw together the dome's meridians, and the sun's rays do not cross it. Fixed in the ground, because this forces the spiral to be upturned, is a humble concave pool, whose compactness must bear the burden of highlighting the meaning of the space that hosts it, conceived as paradox, antinomy—Augustine's "conflict of contrary laws." The spatial anisotropy, the directional dependence, in the museum does not follow the vertical axis, but rather the opposite, expiring in a footprint. The climax of the whole construction does not coincide with the end of an ascent or with a beginning, a central pole, which a logarithmic spiral could never reach, nor with a heterodox keystone or crown at the roof. Instead it culminates in a wet hole, where the spring both winds down and replenishes its energy. The task of sanctioning the height of the construction—of declaring it unequivocally finished and of visibly demonstrating its completion, even proclaiming its otherness with respect to the attestation of ephemeral power that languishes on the city's aerial skyline and is evoked by the symbolic meanings usually attributed to the spiral—was entrusted to the static outline of a band. This band, or rather a massive ring, compresses and crushes the building with its massive weight.

The antinomy represented by the Guggenheim would not benefit from the bulk and eloquence that set it apart if the principal result obtained by the obstinacy of the architect to carry out his project had not been that of bending, until its allegiance was guaranteed, the resistance of an arrogant cohort—time—which, however, rewards those who take care to domesticate it. As we have seen, over the seventeen years Wright dedicated to his chief work, and in particular during the thirty-six months spent building it, time took on different semblances. It would show up as an economic limitation, or bureaucratic and administrative obstacles; at other points it would take on the form of his patrons' vacillations, or the aversion shown by critics, difficulties in building, hostility of public opinion, and then on Wright's side doubt, enthusiasm, disappointment, and hope. It took on the faces of Hilla Rebay and James Johnson Sweeney, of Solomon and Harry Guggenheim, of George Cohen and William Wesley Peters, and many other characters. But then—as Louis Carré had perhaps intuited, without having been able to identify it as the angel of whom he spoke—time turned out to be the architect's most faithful ally. In opposing it, Wright gripped the project in a vise

of relinquishments, until it granted to the building a radical, barbaric essentiality, an unforeseeable coherence. In exchange, the architect acknowledged to time the role of protagonist, making it the object of the experience that his work accomplishes. A flow that is non-absolute, not equal, not univocal over time pervades the inside of the museum. In this space, the movement of the spiral reveals its own interminable reversibility; "reversibility," in the Tantric language studied by Octavio Paz, means that "each word can be converted into its contrary

Interior views immediately following and before the 1959 opening

and later, or simultaneously, turn into itself again." Furthermore, in the Guggenheim the spiral coils around a void, a disconcerting interval. But unlike what Wright had learned while traveling in Japan and reading Okakura, the interval in the Guggenheim is not static; it is a space that expands and narrows, that grows without changing, dynamic, directionless, and like time, can only become; it embraces the silence that traverses it, dissipating its energy in the vacuum that supports it. But in the Guggenheim, the empty space does not equate with absence, and still less is it the result of subtraction or excavation: on the contrary, it coincides with the form of order, opposed to the claims of weight, or gravitas, and necessity. "Order" is the translation of the Greek word *kósmos*, a word that indicates measured and therefore decorated space, removed from the boundless, unornamented matter. Among the meanings of "order" and "ornament" Coomaraswamy wrote of an original connection that is difficult to appreciate for someone who embraces "a provincial view of art, born of a confusion between the (objective) beauty of order and the (subjectively) pleasant." But despite the fact that "we have divorced the 'satis-faction' of the artifact from the artifact itself, and made it seem to be the whole of art," as Coomaraswamy put it, the echo of this link reverberates in the Guggenheim, where geometry and space, calculation and material fuse together, where measurement and ornament belong together, masking internal conflicts.

The events we have covered to this point—contrary to what some historians believe in claiming that they can be attributed to the irreparable upending of Wright's original project and what Jordy called the "awkward" character of the finished building—in fact protected the museum from the excesses that the architect had curried, obliging him to see in superfluity an adversary from which to free himself. Boosting his determination, testing his resoluteness, narrowing the field of choices and alternatives, time stood beside the designer, and now we must recognize the contribution it made to the success of the architect's last venture. Just as the wind sweeps dust off a rock, or a rain shapes and shines its surfaces with slow drips, in the same way time benevolently accompanied the old architect in the last phase of his life, allowing Wright to achieve his masterpiece, an example of timeless architecture and one of the highest expressions of twentieth-century culture.

Chapter Eight
Wright's Iconoclasm

Wright was in New York for the last time in January 1959. On April 3, six days before his death, he wrote from Taliesin West to Medley Whelpley, trustee of the Solomon R. Guggenheim Foundation, exhorting him to "be a good fellow." Specifically, he implored him to intervene so that his project would not be subjected to further alteration, in the form of a gate around the museum, which would have made it appear, he maintained, "guarded as a penitentiary." Fervently he wrote, "We, some of us, would like to see the building as it was designed without desecration." The architect was readying himself to take leave from his work and his clients. Relations with the latter, with the museum director, James Johnson Sweeney, and some of the indecisive trustees of the foundation had significantly deteriorated in recent years. In 1956, his suggestion to give the "memorial in honor of Uncle Sol" the new name, "The Archeseum," struck a nerve with "Lieber Harry" (Harry Guggenheim, chair of the Guggenheim Foundation board), who was aware of the effects that such an explicitly provocative proposal would have produced among the public. In the following months, the dialogue with Sweeney (whom Wright addressed mockingly as "Mein Herr Direktor James") became impossible: "With Sweeney as guide there," he wrote to Harry Guggenheim in December 1958, "we are not safe, as in fact he knows less about architecture in general and our museum building in particular than anyone I ever met."

In this environment, heading for the worst, Wright employed his remaining energy during the last months of his life thwarting the "final touches" the director was pursuing. Sweeney wanted the museum walls to be painted white and demanded that an artificial lighting system be installed. For Wright, white was a "non color," and he had maintained before the trustees in November 1958 that "the old contention by the curator-artificializer in favor of artificial exaggeration of the painting in itself does not compensate for the lost beauty of its relation to the nature of the light in which it was born and the beauty of its environment." Convinced of this, he defended his idea of displaying paintings by leaning them against the inclined walls of the museum spiral, bathed in the light filtering from the skylights above, and not, as Sweeney would mandate, hanging from protruding supports, to present them vertically. Furthermore, taking his cue from what he had observed in Alfred Stieglitz's gallery, An American Place, and recalling how Georgia O'Keeffe had offered to donate her oil painting *Pelvis with Shadows and the Moon* in a simple metallic frame, he argued for eliminating frames, to treat each painting exhibited in the museum (after having removed those celebratory artifacts) as "an individual thing in itself"—separate parts of a mesmerizing, chromatic flux.

Nevertheless, although he had lucidly understood that the requests from Sweeney and his supporters did not stem from simple notions on museum layout that could cause conflict, but instead aimed to restore "the old orthodox-order in the new world we have thus created," subjecting the very conception of the museum to a crude attack, Wright agreed between the end of 1958 and the beginning of 1959 to yet another compromise. To give the foundation's trustees and director a concrete demonstration of what his choices would have brought about concerning the layout of the museum, in April 1958 he presented a series of drawings that show the internal spiral with the furnishings and the paintings fixed to the inclined walls and on movable stands, positioned along the ramp. Emphasizing the presence of sections of the rib vaults, these designs were aimed to demonstrate that it would be possible to make a series of separate spaces within the museum—small, sheltered rooms, traditionally furnished with seats enticingly displayed. It is doubtful that these were effective—useless as they were, with an exaggerated marketing aspect to them, crude in their excessive realism and their obvious instrumentalism. Preparing them was Wright's last recourse to convince his clients and grasp at the possibility of a final mediation. Despite the modest results obtained through this move, at the start of 1959 he turned to Sweeney to ask him for some paintings—"for hanging [as] you like them to be"— along a portion of the ramp. He gave a rough indication of the dimensions of the canvases that he wished to use, and similarly made a broad request for paintings with strong reds, blues, and whites, adding, "I would especially like the one Bauer of a big red globe." This letter from January 14, 1959, three months before the architect's death on April 9, while at first may look unremarkable, was one of the most moving among those in

Sketches showing the outfittings of the
ramps and of the ground floor, 1958

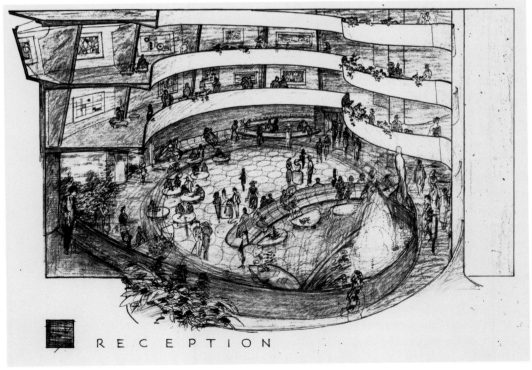

the collection of Wright's Guggenheim correspondence, if we pick up on the allusion. In all likelihood, the painting by Bauer that Wright referred to was *Red Circle* (1930–32). In 1937 it was the cover image for the exhibition catalogue when the Guggenheim collection was shown at the Philadelphia Art Alliance. By asking to display this particular piece, Wright was not making an innocent request, but rather a cryptic signal, subliminally evoking and recalling the origin of the events that would cause the paths of Wright and Sweeney to cross. Doing so, it is fair to suppose, would have also been a melancholic turning back of time, bringing himself back before those decisions he considered unfortunate, before having to turn, broken-spiritedly, to Harry Guggenheim: "I plead with you now not to fail me in completing this work as it was originally conceived," after having informed him, "I am commanded by physicians, wife and friends to sequester myself."

Having retraced the museum's history, and recalled how these words conclude it, we must define what qualities Wright implemented in order to build it: these include shrewdness, prescience, and the ability to adapt in a chameleonlike way—characteristics inherent in the Greek word *Mètis*. This pivotal term indicates a form of technical, astute intelligence required by the architect, who must be a *pantoporos*: someone who is "all-resourceful who is able to find any hole—poros is hole." And like a polymorphous, polyvalent helmsman, he must "[find] a *poros*—a path, a way out, an expedient—to finesse the wind." So too had Wright in the last seventeen years of his life used "these 'machinations,' these *mèchanai* as the Greeks would say—which require a multifaceted intelligence," to cite one of the most wonderful passages in Marcel Detienne's "Le navire d'Athéna."

However, all this does not suffice and does not help to explain the most profound reasons why the construction of the Guggenheim was constantly accompanied by open polemics, and in some cases resentful animosity. After Solomon's death, criticism of Wright's project intensified. When in 1956 the *New York Times* aired the reservations that twenty-one prominent artists had about the museum project, as we have seen, the long-term campaign against the plans announced and pursued by Solomon Guggenheim and, especially, by Hilla Rebay came to a climax. Already in April 1951 the *New York Times* maintained that for "the interests of the public, artists and modern art" it would be opportune to turn over the construction of the new museum and Solomon Guggenheim's bequest to two existing New York museums—MoMA and the Whitney. The opinions reflected in this article led Harry Guggenheim to attempt to reassure the public. Guaranteeing his own involvement to tone down Rebay's "radical plans" in favor of "a more flexible artistic form than the present one," he too showed that he was not indifferent to the prejudice of the New York bon ton, which thought itself maker and guardian of the "creation of the value of the 'new'" as Harold Rosenberg put it, whose customs, tastes, rituals, and objectives did not agree with the plans Guggenheim and Rebay had conceived, and which Wright translated into the form of the museum. Another episode of the debate, fanned by the press, which shared those points of view and supported the solid interests underlying them, deserves our attention. Despite her later appreciation for Wright's building, in 1954 Aline Louchheim voiced the suspicion that the Guggenheim Foundation was an esoteric and occult place, "inclined to mysticism," "unrelated." This blunt platitude was aimed mostly at Rebay since, during her life—or "lives"—the baroness did not conceal her interest in Theosophy, the theories of Rudolf Steiner and Madame Blavatsky, or the fact that she had studied Eastern religions, as was not unusual among the people she associated with during her youth. Inevitably, such an accusation would also strike Wright's project. The curiosity and conjectures that the project continued to raise were obviously not without basis: as early as 1943 the Guggenheim spoke an unfamiliar tongue, the "language of the Other," which would have sounded "obscure" and heavy with disturbing and "mystical" intentions—in short, "barbarian." But, if "barbarian" is freed of its derogatory connotations, and its true meaning is evoked, it is a perfectly apt term for the Guggenheim. "Barbarian" is an onomatopoeic term tracing back to "stuttering"; originally the label singled out the stranger and was set aside for the stutterer who attempted to make his identity known to his host (*hospes*). This effort to communicate one's identity meant that over time "barbarian" became "foreigner," and from the shared root of *hospes* and *hostis*, "host" became a synonym for "enemy." In consequence, the "exoticism" borne by the foreigner took on the meaning of a disreputable, dangerous difference, a result that the changing sense of the words describes, and in some ways helps us to understand the fate of the Guggenheim and the work carried out by Wright.

Just as the barbarian's stuttering elicited scorn and derision, exoticism was accepted by Modernists solely for laughs, like some bizarre or extravagant act to confirm the multifaceted ways in which novelty propagates itself. Suffering from an analogous evolution, no longer accompanied step-by-step by those who had created it, the collection assembled by Guggenheim and Rebay was transformed into yet another museum; and as in every museum, the meaning each object holds is presented as an attribute of history, and history is presented as a fetish. At the same time, Wright's building became a curious attraction, an object whose purpose is attested by a reassuring willingness to let itself be carried by the ocean's waves, uncrossable without an intelligent helmsman to guide it in the "right direction," or *ithynein*, to paraphrase Detienne.

The Guggenheim could not but appear "exotic," "barbarian," and "unrelated" to those following the liturgy that was developed for the worship of art—of which Sweeney was a high priest. His task was to render the Guggenheim a museum analogous and similar to his previous workplace, the Museum of Modern Art, and with this compete for the prize of the public's favor. Wright fully grasped one of the most obvious implications, and even wrote to the director of the Guggenheim in February 1958, "I now see the hopeless schism between the museum-as-a-business competing-with-other-museums that is your ambition to run and the amenities of the *memorial-museum* Mr. Guggenheim made his bequest to build and himself went through with his architect step by step." A "museum-as-a-business" is an expression that evokes a section of *The Arcades Project*, in which Walter Benjamin observes that "there exist relations between the department store and the museum, between which the bazaar creates a mediating link." Constructing the Guggenheim as a walled space against which the waves of clichés would crash, Wright was determined to protect the works of art conserved within it from the common fate Benjamin described: "amass[ed] in the museums," appearing like "commodities, which—where they offer themselves en masse to the passerby—awake in him the notion that some part of this should fall to him as well." In the modern era, the museum had become not only the last oasis for the bourgeois need for security and inclusion; it was also a powerful instrument at the disposal of the cultural industry, which debases all who "participate in the game as simple consumers to exploit," as Hans Georg Gadamer observed. By using the "masterpiece" to jolt the public, museums lead their visitors to

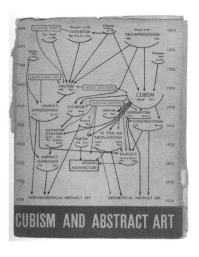

Catalogue cover for the 1936 exhibition *Cubism and Abstract Art* at the Museum of Modern Art, by Alfred H. Barr Jr.

"see, in the encounter with the work of art, a simple rapture or enchantment, that is a simple liberation from the pressure of reality and enjoyment of a fake freedom," if we trust this optimistic belief. This is not, however, the reason our museums have ceased to be crass institutions, as Rainer Maria Rilke said half a century before the events that occupy us, in his *Florentine Diaries*, "As if someone blindly tore pages out of different books in different languages and pasted them together into one huge luxury volume. These are our museums." The brushstrokes of this crassness are imbued with the dedication to collecting—experiencing its most prurient expansion and producing the most spectacular and admirable results in the United States. "Years ago I decided that the greatest need of our Country was art as we were a very young country," Isabella Stewart Gardner wrote to Edmund Hill in 1917, being Mrs. Jack, herself one of the most inspired architects of that form of devotion. For America, history was an exogenous and exotic flower, as Jean Baudrillard has put it. Similar to the present day, but on a rather broader track, at the time of Isabella Stewart Gardner and Pierpont Morgan, to win that flower "wealthy Americans criss-crossed the Atlantic on their private steam yachts, in search of everything Europe had to offer," wrote Wayne Craven, "from fashionable Parisian gowns by Worth to titled husbands for their daughters, from rare Botticelli Madonnas to whole rooms from noble palazzos or hoary castles."

When the Guggenheim was being built, Abby Rockefeller and Alfred Barr led the group of descendants of this tradition, described much earlier by Henry James. The object of their desires was no longer the works of Bellini, Titian, or Velázquez resplendent in so many American museums, but the Future. It was no coincidence that one year before the death of Solomon Guggenheim, in 1948, Abby Rockefeller had included in her will a clause obliging MoMA to pass on to the Metropolitan Museum and the Art Institute of Chicago paintings which were past their prime. As Karsten Schubert noted, the wife of John D. Rockefeller Jr. had explicit ideas regarding the mission of the institution she had helped to create. Alfred Barr, who had conceived the MoMA project with the attitude of a Darwinist entomologist, interpreted its meaning with an image tinged with Futurist tones, comparing MoMA's collections to a torpedo, "its head the ever-advancing present, its tail the ever-receding past of 50 to 100 years ago." Seeing the future as the present's only

"Torpedo. Diagram of the Ideal Permanent Collection" drawn by Alfred H. Barr Jr., 1933

hope, which otherwise was destined to extinguish itself in the past, what Barr and friends envisioned coincided with a definitive distancing from Baudelaire and from the idea that "the art of each epoch aspires to obtain the dignity of that which came before" (Jean Clair). When the Guggenheim was inaugurated, the liturgy that had taken root had found a reliable new place of worship. Thus it is not surprising that in visiting the museum when it had finally been set up and furnished, Rebay was disconsolate and offended by it; she felt the collection was displayed in a muddled sequence of "isms," periods, artists, and styles—a betrayal of what she had done in developing Solomon Guggenheim's collection.

It would be reductive and naïve to think that all this can be explained by the failure of communication that developed between the builder of the museum and the one given the task of directing it. Wright's claim that speaking with Sweeney about architectural matters produced the same results as "trying to persuade a New York Irish policeman that St. Patrick was English" was merely a spirited barb. Other expressions he used in referring to the long confrontation with Sweeney were: "orthodox order," "the artificial exaggeration of the painting," "glassification of picture," and summed up in two words, "old school." Still more explicit is this passage from a letter he sent to Sweeney in January 1959: "The honor of our museum it will more and more consist in the abolition of the 'rectilinear frame of reference' (the limitation of the carpenter). This new museum defying the 'authority' of orthodox dispensation is not yet fully comprehended by the professionals. The 'Guggenheim' still in danger from orthodox 'authority.'" In these words the

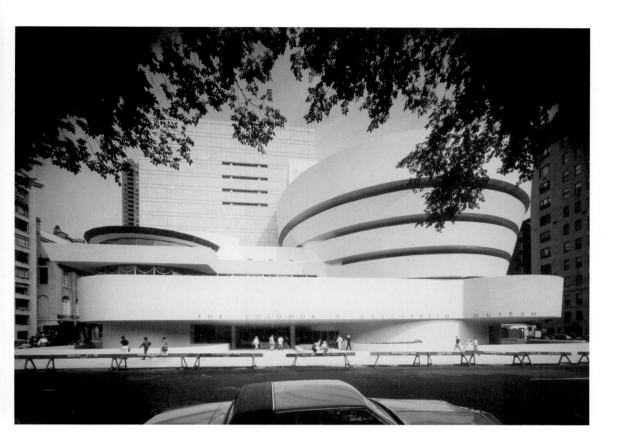

Guggenheim Museum, view from Fifth Avenue, c. 1995. The addition built by Siegel and Associates in 1992 can be seen in the background.

conviction that orthodoxy makes authority dangerous and devoid re-emerges: as we have seen in these pages, this is the driving concept behind Wright's thought, the backbone of his work, and here is the explanation of why he always identified his architecture with the word "Democracy." Unlike what had happened many times in history, it was not the power of the images that Wright attacked, and the history of the Guggenheim does not display merely another conflict between art and architecture. What inspired the Guggenheim project, with ever greater clarity as years went on, was the refusal to make architecture subservient to the worship of the images—a devotion that would have depleted the power of the architecture. To avoid any misunderstanding, and at the risk of being redundant, this means that in Wright's case, iconoclasm was not aimed at the images but at the forms of worship that made art its object. In this sense, its iconoclasm was different from

Aerial view of the Guggenheim Museum from above Central Park

any other ancient form. Iconoclasm, in this case, does not affirm the impossibility of representing in a material, circumscribed form what is divinely immaterial and uncircumscribable (following David Freedberg), but rather is synonymous with the refusal to conceive the use of images in the aim of attributing to them a power over the viewer, and rejecting the superstitions that this use generates.

Words that can describe the Guggenheim's iconoclasm are not to be found among ancient Greek terms, nor among those used by the Byzantine iconoclast faction. There is nothing aniconic in this construction. In the majestic and perfectly iconic space of the Guggenheim, it is not possible to notice the echo of the great European iconoclasm, of the words of Swingli or of Luther, for example. The iconoclasm of the Guggenheim takes aim at the modern *superstitions* (very similar to those Erasmus described with scathing irony in his *In Praise of Folly*) which our museums favor. And in large part these superstitions have even set the pace for the history we have recounted.

Portfolio of
Photographs,
Drawings, and
References

Gordon Strong Automobile Objective and Planetarium, Sugarloaf Mountain, Maryland, 1924–25

Conceptual sketch, elevation, and perspective, 1924

Morris Gift Shop, San Francisco, California, 1948–50

Entrance and partial view of the interior

S. C. Johnson & Son Administration Building, 1936–39, and Johnson Research Tower, 1943–50, Racine, Wisconsin

Administration Building, interior

Solomon R. Guggenheim Museum, New York, 1943–59

Perspective and plan drawings of a design featuring galleries distributed on separate hexagonal floors

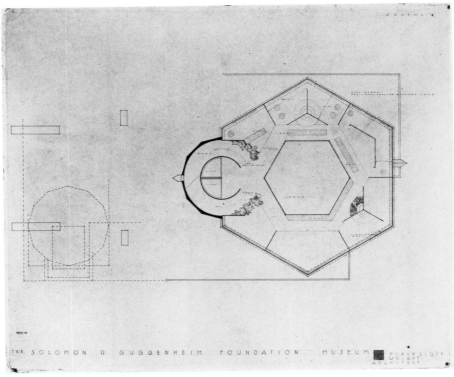

Perspective drawings with the diminishing and inverted spirals and red exterior, 1943–44

Elevation and perspective drawings of
the inverted spiral design, 1944

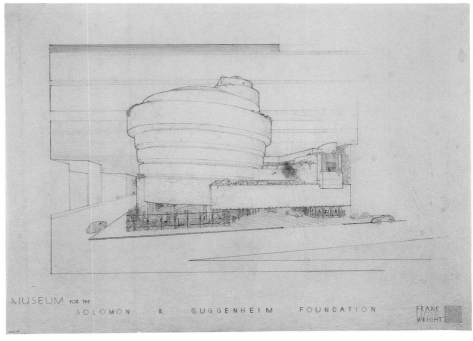

MUSEUM FOR THE
SOLOMON R GUGGENHEIM FOUNDATION

FRANK
LLOYD
WRIGHT

Section; section with the Ocular
Chamber; detail of the observatory, 1944

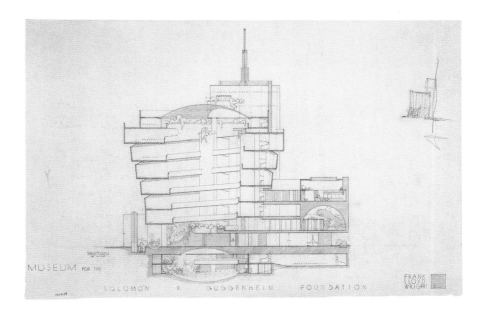

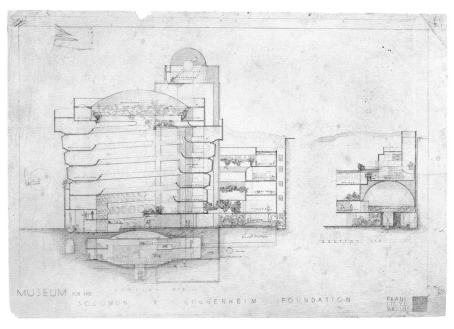

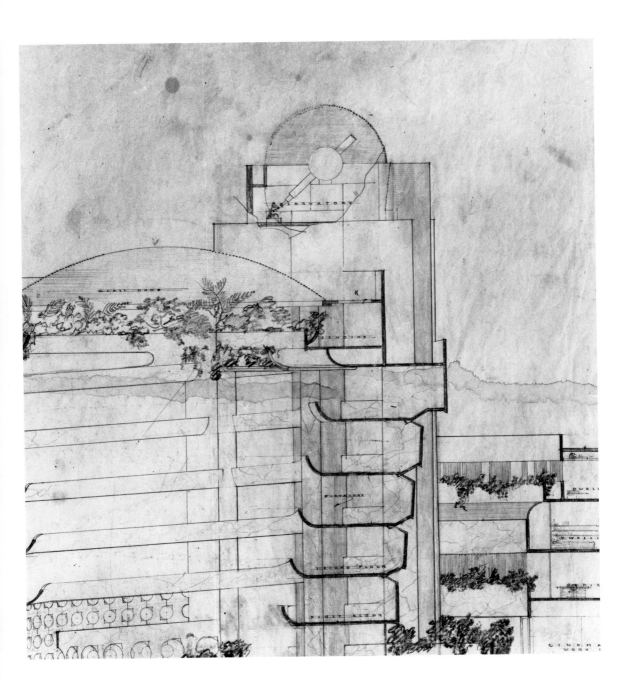

Ground floor plan, with the word
"ZIGGURAT" written at lower right

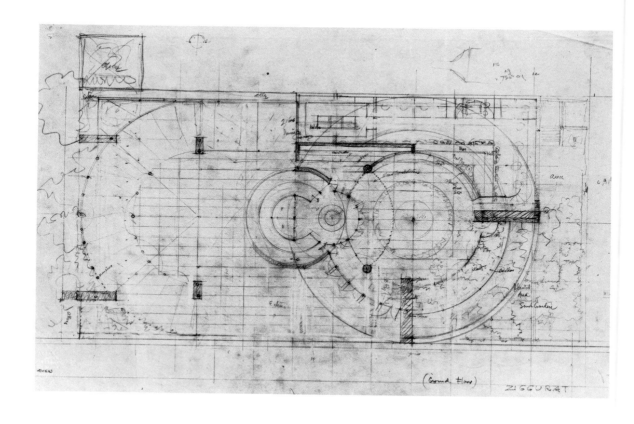

Ground floor plan

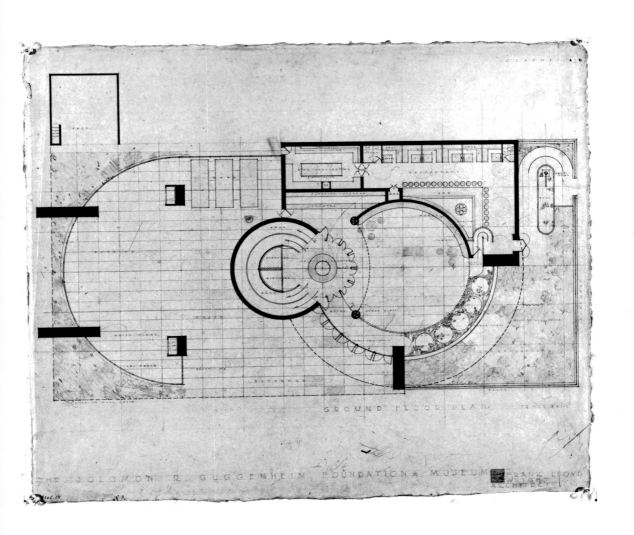

MUSEUM FOR THE SOLOMON R. GUGGENHEIM FOUNDATION
FRANK LLOYD WRIGHT ARCHITECT

THE MODERN GALLERY
MEMORIAL MUSEUM FOR THE SOLOMON R GUGGENHEIM FOUNDATION
FRANK LLOYD WRIGHT ARCHITECT

Perspective drawings, 1948, 1951, 1953

The Modern Gallery. Ground floor plan,
1945

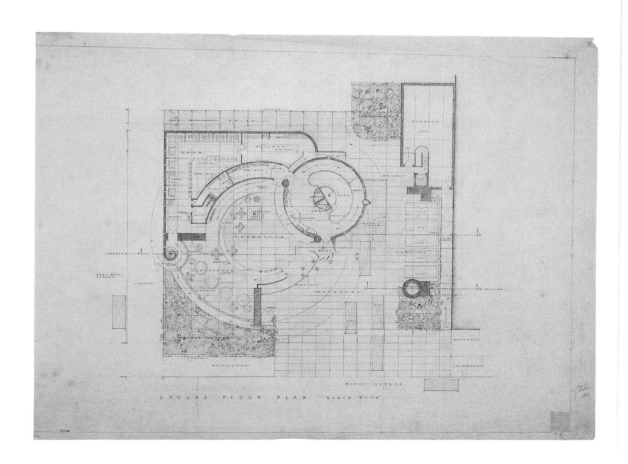

Presentation of the model of the Modern Gallery, New York, 1945. Hilla Rebay, Solomon Guggenheim, and Frank Lloyd Wright are seated at the second table on the left.

> Model of the Modern Gallery, 1945

Model of the Modern Gallery with the addition of the Annex, 1947

The Modern Gallery. Plan of the ground floor showing the addition of the Annex, 1947; plan of the ground floor, 1952

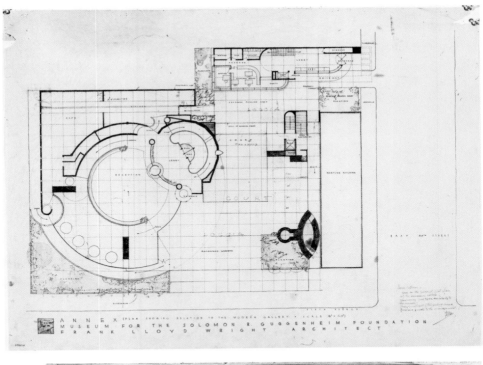

ANNEX (PLAN SHOWING RELATION TO THE MODERN GALLERY) SCALE 16"=1'0"
MUSEUM FOR THE SOLOMON R. GUGGENHEIM FOUNDATION
FRANK LLOYD WRIGHT ARCHITECT

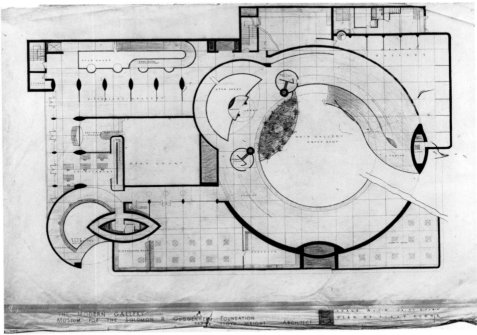

THE MODERN GALLERY
MUSEUM FOR THE SOLOMON R. GUGGENHEIM FOUNDATION
LLOYD WRIGHT ARCHITECT

SCALE 16"=1'0"
PLAN OF FIRST FLOOR

Section drawing, with separate details
showing the ramp and the exterior wall in
section, 1953–54

Plan of the second floor, 1953–54

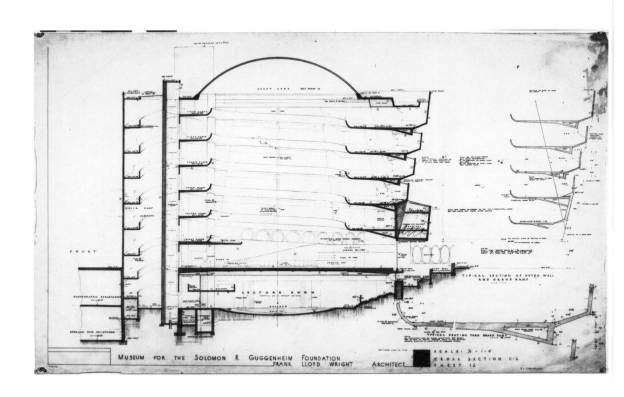

MUSEUM FOR THE SOLOMON R GUGGENHEIM FOUNDATION
FRANK LLOYD WRIGHT ARCHITECT

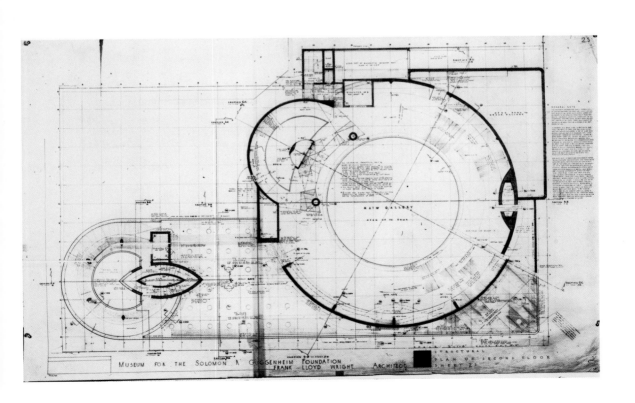

MUSEUM FOR THE SOLOMON R GUGGENHEIM FOUNDATION
FRANK LLOYD WRIGHT ARCHITECT

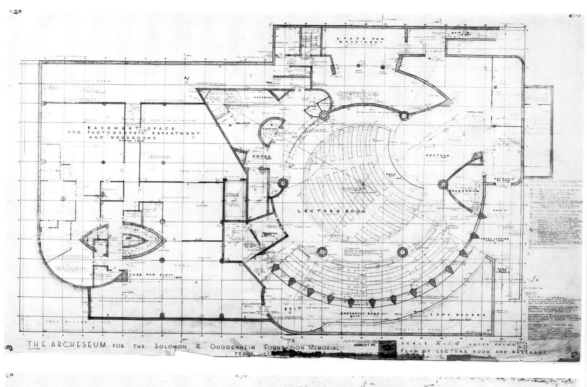

THE ARCHESEUM FOR THE SOLOMON R GUGGENHEIM FOUNDATION MEMORIAL
FRANK L.
SCALE ⅛″ = 1′-0″
PLAN OF LECTURE ROOM AND BASEMENT

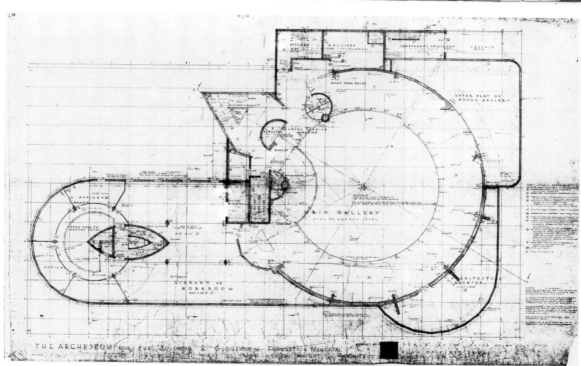

THE ARCHESEUM FOR THE SOLOMON R GUGGENHEIM FOUNDATION MEMORIAL
FRANK LLOYD WRIGHT ARCHITECT
SCALE ⅛″ = 1′-0″
PLAN OF FIRST

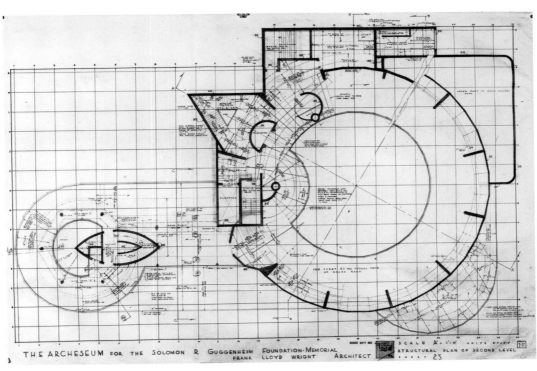

THE ARCHESEUM FOR THE SOLOMON R GUGGENHEIM FOUNDATION·MEMORIAL FRANK LLOYD WRIGHT ARCHITECT   SCALE ⅛"=1'-0" UNITS _____   STRUCTURAL PLAN OF SECOND LEVEL   SHEET 25

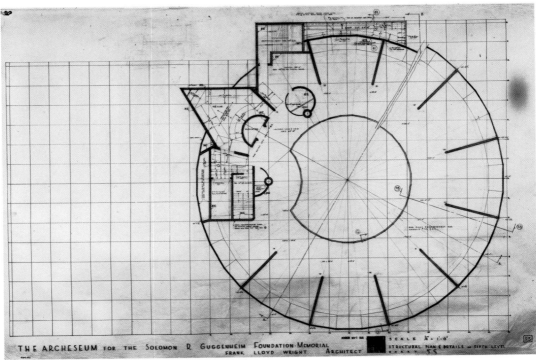

THE ARCHESEUM FOR THE SOLOMON R GUGGENHEIM FOUNDATION·MEMORIAL FRANK LLOYD WRIGHT ARCHITECT   SCALE ⅛"=1'-0"   STRUCTURAL PLAN & DETAILS OF FIFTH LEVEL   SHEET 35

< The Archeseum. Plan drawings of the
auditorium, ground floor, second floor,
and fifth floor, 1956

The Archeseum. Section on the main axis
(to the right of the ramp), 1956; section
on the minor axis (to the right of the
skylight), 1956

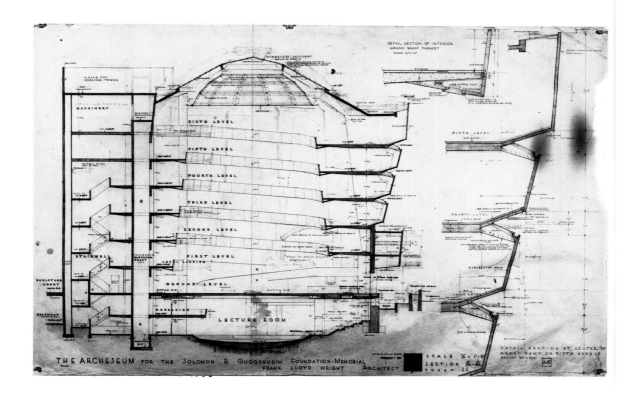

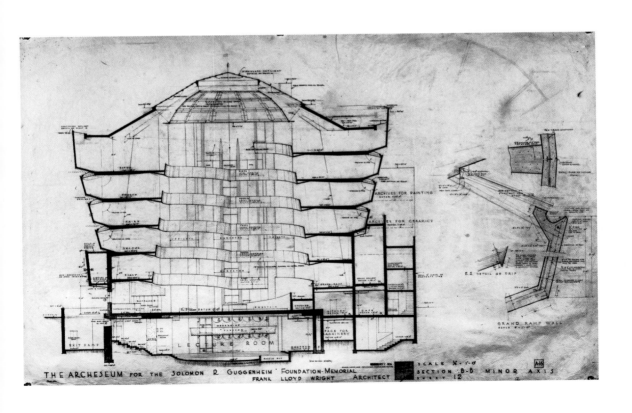

THE ARCHESEUM FOR THE SOLOMON R GUGGENHEIM FOUNDATION-MEMORIAL
FRANK LLOYD WRIGHT ARCHITECT

SCALE ⅛=1-0
SECTION B-B MINOR AXIS
SHEET 12

The Archeseum. Section and elevation of
the Guggenheim Foundation's offices,
1956; west elevation, 1956; presentation
perspective drawing, 1956

The Guggenheim Museum. Plan of the
ground floor, 1958

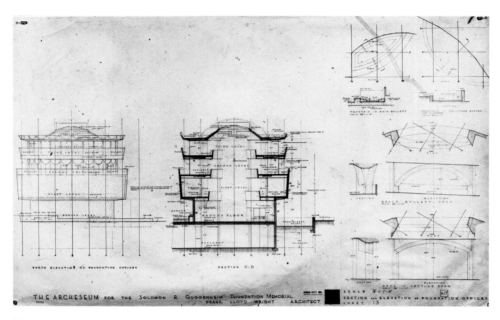

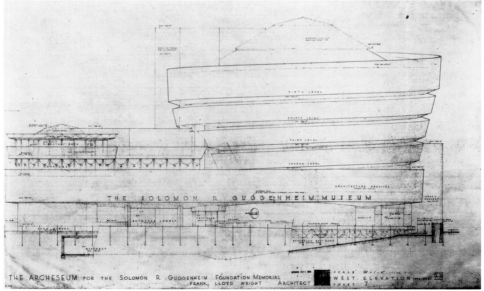

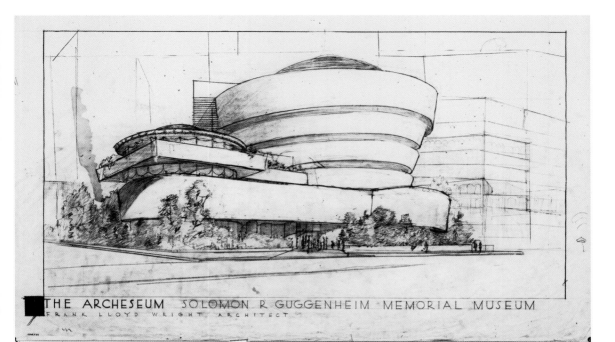

THE ARCHESEUM SOLOMON R GUGGENHEIM MEMORIAL MUSEUM
FRANK LLOYD WRIGHT ARCHITECT

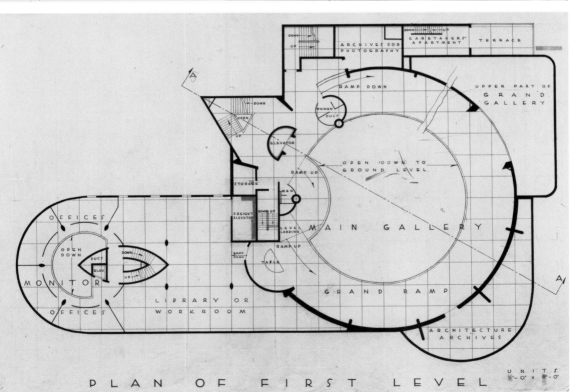

PLAN OF FIRST LEVEL

The Archeseum. Structural drawings of
the cupola's glass roof, 1954

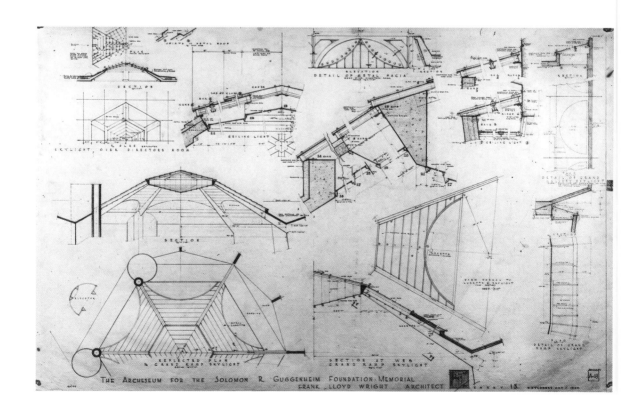

Studies for the cupola's glass roof, c. 1958

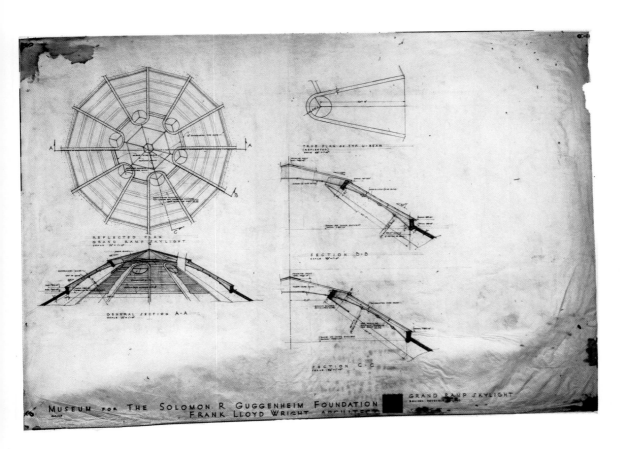

LOOKING DOWN INTO LOBBY

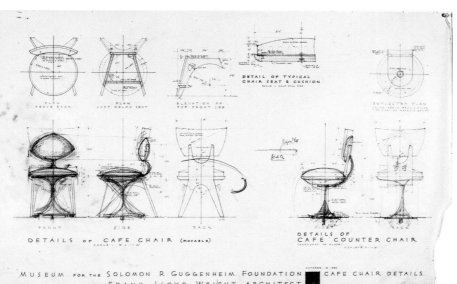

DETAIL OF TYPICAL
CHAIR SEAT & CUSHION

DETAILS OF CAFE CHAIR (MOVABLE)

DETAILS OF
CAFE COUNTER CHAIR

MUSEUM FOR THE SOLOMON R GUGGENHEIM FOUNDATION CAFE CHAIR DETAILS
FRANK LLOYD WRIGHT ARCHITECT

Sketch of the lobby, c. 1957

Sketches of the chairs for the cafeteria, 1957

Studies for the gallery screens, 1959

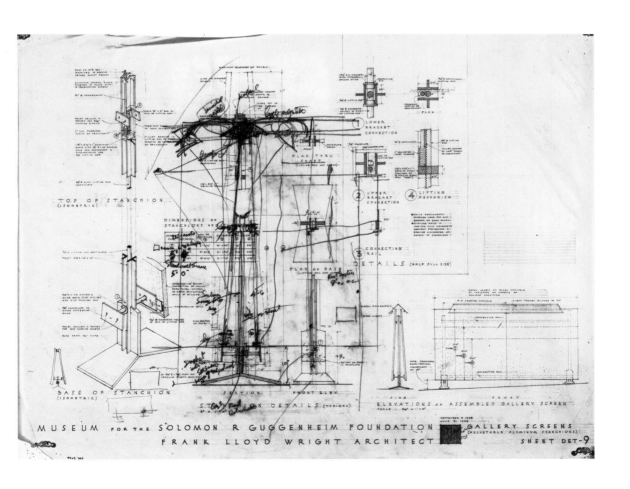

② S.E. COR. FIFTH AVE. & E. 89TH ST.
JAN. 11. 1951

SITE

FIFTH AVE.

④ FIFTH AVE. FACING NORTH
FROM 100 FT. SOUTH OF E. 88 ST.
JAN. 11. 1951.

E. 88 ST.

FIFTH AVE.

The site of the Guggenheim Museum,
southeast corner of Fifth Avenue and
89th Street, January 11, 1951

Fifth Avenue near the future site of the
Guggenheim Museum, January 11, 1951

Building the Guggenheim's "drum," 1957

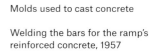

Molds used to cast concrete

Welding the bars for the ramp's reinforced concrete, 1957

Building the floor of the lobby, 1958

Construction of the structure of the glass
cupola and the final shape of the
"hairpins," 1958

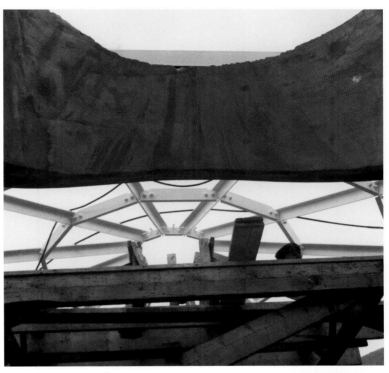

The Guggenheim Museum between 1958
and 1960

The auditorium

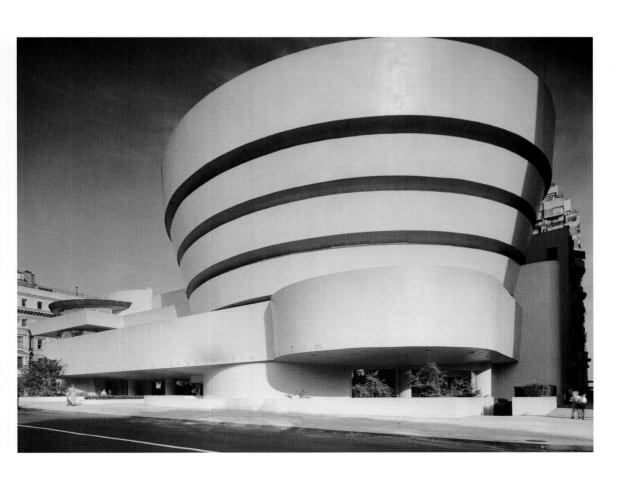

Bibliographical Note

Since in the pages of this book images have partially taken the place of footnotes, I feel that I owe the reader some explanations. I hope that the most demanding readers, interested in delving deeper into the study of Wright's work, will welcome this information as friendly suggestions.

The first version of this book was published in Italian in 2004. What you hold in your hands has more or less the same structure, with some inevitable modifications and clarifications. Between 2003 and 2016 the literature dedicated to the matters I discussed grew significantly, and in the pages that follow I have included the references to the publications I consulted in the definitive writing of the book.

The archives I consulted are those of the Solomon R. Guggenheim Museum in New York and of the Frank Lloyd Wright Foundation in Scottsdale, Arizona (the archives from the latter are now in New York City, held at the Museum of Modern Art and the Avery Library of Columbia University). In the early 2000s, I made the visit to the Frank Lloyd Wright Archives in Taliesin West that could not be avoided by any researcher interested in Wright's architecture; in addition to a tremendous number of documents conserved there, 859 drawings related to the Guggenheim project are in the collection. Margo Stipe and Bruce Brooks Pfeiffer facilitated the work I carried out in Scottsdale, and I owe them particular gratitude. The Solomon R. Guggenheim Museum has a first-rate photograph library and an excellent archive, which I was able to access thanks to the kindness of Kimberly Bush. I am much indebted to her, as well as to Erica Stoller, who generously let me view and use the photographs held in the Esto archives.

To understand what was held in these and other archives relating to Wright's activities, I let myself be guided by the book edited by P. J. Meehan, *Frank Lloyd Wright: A Research Guide to Archival Sources* (1983). Among the bibliographic instruments, repertories, and works of a general nature from which I took my cue, notable are: R. L. Sweeney, *Frank Lloyd Wright: An Annotated Bibliography* (1978); A. A. Storrer, *The Frank Lloyd Wright Companion* (1993); the monumental indices of the correspondence conserved at Taliesin, *Frank Lloyd Wright: An Index to the Taliesin Correspondence* (1988), published by A. Alofsin; the vast photographic documentation of Wright's works contained in the twelve volumes of *Frank Lloyd Wright* (1984–88), edited by B. B. Pfeiffer and Y. Futagawa; and the collection of Wright's texts, also edited by Pfeiffer, *Frank Lloyd Wright: Collected Writings* (1992–95).

Among the several biographies of Wright, those by N. Kelly Smith (*Frank Lloyd Wright: A Study in Architectural Content*, 1979), R. C. Twombly (*Frank Lloyd Wright: His Life and His Architecture*, 1979), and B. Gill (*Many Masks: A Life of Frank Lloyd Wright*, 1987) were the first ones I visited in preparing the lectures I gave, so many years ago, at the Istituto Universitario di Architettura di Venezia. Later, I drew further biographic information from E. Tafel, *About Wright: An Album of Recollections by Those Who Knew Frank Lloyd Wright* (1993), and R. McCarter, *Frank Lloyd Wright* (2006).

For those who wish to become acquainted with Wright's work in general, and the ways in which authoritative scholars have studied it, I recommend four books in particular; published a few decades apart, they also make it possible to gauge the evolution of studies devoted to Wright over the course of more than fifty years. The first is H.-R. Hitchcock's *In the Nature of Materials: The Buildings of Frank Lloyd Wright, 1887–1941* (1942); the second is V. Scully's *Frank Lloyd Wright* (1960); the last two are *The Architecture of Frank Lloyd Wright* (1996) and *The Urbanism of Frank Lloyd Wright* (2016), both by N. Levine. These last two volumes were the most useful to me and naturally are the most up-to-date. Moreover, as I hope will be clear from what I have written, I have for many years found it essential in dealing with Wright and his works to read closely, among his many writings, his own book *The Japanese Print: An Interpretation*, first published in 1912.

Concerning the study of how the Guggenheim was designed and built, *Frank Lloyd Wright, the Guggenheim Correspondence* (1986), edited by Pfeiffer, is essential reading; nearly all the quotations I have used from the letters written by Wright and his clients and other correspondents over the seventeen years he worked on the Guggenheim come from this book, which contains documentation of a sort that one does not often have access to during research, and which compels a stimulating exercise of interpretation. Correspondence is without doubt an indispensible resource for studying Wright's work. In the three volumes edited by Pfeiffer, *F. Ll. Wright, Letters to Apprentices*, *Letters to Architects*, *Letters to Clients*

(1982, 1984, 1986, respectively), there are numerous passages devoted to the Guggenheim project; *Letters to Clients*, for example, contains some of his correspondence with Hibbard Johnson, while in *Letters to Architects* there are also those addressed to H. Th. Wijdeveld and Hitchcock that I have quoted.

Among Wright's many declarations concerning the Guggenheim, those published in the articles and essays "The Modern Gallery" (*Architectural Forum,* January 1946), "The Modern Gallery for the Solomon R. Guggenheim Foundation" (*Magazine of Art,* January 1946), and "An Experiment in the Third-Dimension" (in *The Solomon R. Guggenheim Museum: Frank Lloyd Wright,* 1960) are easily accessible and useful. (See also Pfeiffer, *Frank Lloyd Wright: Collected Writings*, vol. 5 [1994], as well as the typewritten manuscript, to be read with a dose of circumspection, "The Story of the Solomon R. Guggenheim Memorial-Museum," once held at the archives of Taliesin West [MS 2401.389].)

The Solomon Guggenheim Museum (1994) contains an incisive and well-illustrated essay by Pfeiffer. He reconstructs the building phases of the museum and evolution of the project, regarding which there remain some questions that neither the designs nor the records from the various restoration projects can answer. Moreover, Pfeiffer's essay has a passage concerning the "superpositions," so to speak, of the research carried out by Wright and Le Corbusier on the theme of spiral-form constructions, a subject I have dwelt on and which I consider noteworthy. In this book I have dealt on two occasions with the reasons and circumstances, different but not independent if one looks closely, regarding Le Corbusier's role in the history of the Guggenheim. J. Siry drew my attention to an essay by F. Kiesler, "Art and Architecture: Notes on the Spiral Theme in Recent Architecture," in *Partisan Review* (Winter 1946), now in *Frederick J. Kiesler: Selected Writings*, ed. S. Gohr and G. Luyken (1996). This text compares for the first time, as far as I am aware, the projects for the Modern Gallery and the Musée Mondial. N. Levine, in *The Urbanism of Frank Lloyd Wright*, wrote a particularly intelligent discussion of how the project for Wright's Broadacre City was also the result of engaging with Le Corbusier's planning ideas. Read in the light of the Kahn Lectures Wright gave at Princeton University in 1930, later published in the book *Modern Architecture* (1931, re-edited and with an introduction by N. Levine, 2008) and his review of the English edition of Le Corbusier's *Vers une architecture* (Wright, "Towards a New Architecture," *World Unity* 2, no. 6 [1928], now in *The Collected Writings of Frank Lloyd Wright*, vol. 1), Levine's comments played an important role in guiding my interpretation of the Guggenheim. Among the letters written by Le Corbusier, the one he sent to his mother from London on June 3, 1939, which I cited, can be found in *Le Corbusier Correspondance: Lettres à la famille*, edited by R. Baudoui and A. Dercelles, vol. 2 (2013). On that occasion, Le Corbusier spoke of his imminent meeting with Solomon Guggenheim, providing insight the implications of which are yet to be clarified.

In tracing the history of the museum, I turned to the Guggenheim's official "catalogue": *Art of This Century: The Guggenheim Museum and Its Collection* (1993). This volume is well researched and comprehensively illustrated, and it includes contributions by C. Bell, J. Brown, L. Dennison, A. Feeser, N. Spector, as well as those which served me the most, in different ways: T. Krens, "The Genesis of a Museum"; M. Gowan, "Technology and the Spirit," dedicated to the origin of the idea of non-objective painting; J. Blessing, "Peggy's Surreal Playground"; and D. Waldman, "Art of This Century and the New York School." Important updates concerning the museum's history can be found in *The Guggenheim: Frank Lloyd Wright and the Making of the Modern Museum* (2009), with essays of varying depth by H. Ballon, L. E. Carranza, Pfeiffer, P. Kirkham and S. W. Perkins, Levine, Siry, N. Spector, A. Starita, G. Zuaznabar, and a well-constructed chronology. In addition to these, the publications I drew information and suggestions from were: chapter 10, in particular, of Levine's monograph *The Architecture of Frank Lloyd Wright* (noted above); the essay by K. Frampton published in the volume edited by T. Riley and P. Reed, *Frank Lloyd Wright Architect* (1994); chapter 5 of the volume by W. H. Jordy, *American Buildings and Their Architects: The Impact of European Modernism in the Mid-Twentieth Century* (1972).

The most precise studies devoted to the building solutions and construction techniques implemented in making the museum, the analysis of which has critically influenced the structure of my book, were those by T. Trombetti, "Il funzionamento strutturale del Guggenheim Museum di Frank Lloyd Wright," *Casabella* (November 2007); the chapter "The Guggenheim Refigured" in S. Allen's *Practice: Architecture, Technique + Representation* (2009); and the following essays by

Siry: "Wright's Guggenheim Museum and Late Modernist Architecture," in the 2009 collaborative book *The Guggenheim: Frank Lloyd Wright and the Making of the Modern Museum*; "The Spiral Ramped Floor in Wright's Guggenheim Museum," in R. Gargiani (ed.), *L'architrave, le plancher, la plate-forme: Nouvelle histoire de la construction* (2012); and, above all, "Seamless Continuity *versus* the Nature of Materials," which appeared in the *Journal of the Society of Architectural Historians* (March 2012). This last essay contains not only a meticulous analysis of the building system used by Wright but also an exhaustive series of bibliographic references. Among these references, I devote a special attention to G. N. Cohen, "Frank Lloyd Wright's Guggenheim Museum," *Concrete Construction* (March 1958); C. W. Spero, "Forms Mold Sculptured Concrete Museum," *Construction Methods and Equipment* (April 1958), and "Spiral Museum Is Built Like Work of Art," *Engineering News-Record* (December 5, 1957). Moreover, I was able to find information regarding the engineers who worked with Wright in J. Quinan's essay, "L'ingegneria e gli ingegneri di Frank Lloyd Wright," *Casabella* (April 1958).

Many articles published in the *New York Times* in the 1950s help give an idea of New Yorkers' opinions of Wright's project, a theme that surfaces a few times in these pages. Among these articles, I would like to highlight: "21 Artists Assail Museum Interior" (December 12, 1956); A. Saarinen, "Tour with Mr. Wright" (September 22, 1957); J. Canaday, "Wright vs. Painting" (October 21, 1959); and A. L. Huxtable, "That Museum: Wright or Wrong?" (October 25, 1959).

The October 1, 1945, issue of *Time* magazine contains an article titled "Optimistic Ziggurat" that attributes a sense of optimism (credited to Wright), on the one hand, and pessimism on the other (N. Levine has also discussed the matter) to which the opposing developments of the Guggenheim's spiral is probably due. It is a subject that seems useful to note, but that I have avoided. Among the articles that appeared in the international press following the inauguration of the museum, it is worth mentioning (though little can be learned from reading them): E. Kaufmann Jr., "The Form of Space for Art: Guggenheim Museum," *Art in America* (Winter 1959–60); P. Blake, "The Guggenheim Museum: Museum or Monument?" *Architectural Forum* (December 1959); H.-R. Hitchcock, "Notes of a Traveller: Wright and Kahn," *Zodiac*, no. 6 (1960). W. J. Hennessey's article "Frank Lloyd Wright and the Guggenheim

Museum," *Arts* (April 1978), unlike those just noted, was the result of original archival research.

To research the relations between Wright and New York, as well as with New York's intellectual, artistic, and high society, I turned to H. Muschamp's book *Man about Town: Frank Lloyd Wright in New York City* (1983) and that of J. Hession and D. Pickrel, *Frank Lloyd Wright in New York* (2007); these were useful, in particular, for evaluating the significant energy expended by Wright during the 1950s in order to engage the support of public opinion and among the city's elite.

In discussing the development of the museum project, I availed myself of M. Reinberger's "The Sugarloaf Mountain Project and Frank Lloyd Wright's Vision of a New World," *Journal of the Society of Architectural Historians* (March 1984); D. De Long's *Frank Lloyd Wright Designs for an American Landscape* (1996); and J. Lipman's *Frank Lloyd Wright and the Johnson Wax Building* (1986). These publications provided what I find to be the best contributions for knowledge of the projects and works that represent the two most pertinent antecedents for the Guggenheim Museum. M. Hertzenberg's book *Wright in Racine* (2004) is a compilation but is well illustrated. Although not driven by analytical intent, P. V. Turner's pages on San Francisco's Morris Shop in *Frank Lloyd Wright and San Francisco* (2016) deserve attention, especially because they contain reproductions of some remarkable drawings.

I believe that Lewis Mumford and Frank Lloyd Wright— as others would concur—were two intellectual protagonists, and not solely for the history of twentieth-century American architecture. For this reason, I preferred to include Mumford's stances with regard to Wright's work, putting them before those of other historians and critics. Among the different articles by Mumford that I have referred to, I find the most significant to be "What Wright Hath Wrought," published in the *New Yorker* (December 5, 1959; included in Mumford, *The Highway and the City* [1963]). To understand the complexity of the relations between Wright and Mumford, their correspondence, published in a book edited by Pfeiffer and R. Wojtowicz, *Frank Lloyd Wright and Lewis Mumford: Thirty Years of Correspondence* (2001), is essential. I would recommend to those interested in this correspondence reading it in the light of Wojtowicz's *Lewis Mumford and American Modernism* (1998) and the collected writings, also edited by Wojtowicz, *Sidewalk Critic: Lewis Mumford's Writings on New York* (1998). What

Mumford himself told me when I met him in 1971, when I was in the United States on a Fulbright Scholarship, goes well beyond the subjects in these books; I took notes from our meetings that I rely on to this day.

The history of the Guggenheim is intimately entwined with that of the Museum of Modern Art. Wright, as I hope emerges clearly from the pages of this book, perceived with particular lucidity the difficult implications of this intertwinedness. To understand the reasons for it, beyond what can commonly be learned through consulting the literature listed below, the book edited by P. Reed and W. Kaizen, which also contains an essay by K. Smith and rich documentary support, *The Show to End All Shows: Frank Lloyd Wright and the Museum of Modern Art, 1940* (2004), is highly recommended. For my regular references to MoMA, no stranger to me, there are of course the studies devoted to Ludwig Mies van der Rohe and Philip Johnson. In particular, I made use of these: H. S. Bee and M. Elligot (eds.), *Art of Our Time: A Chronicle of the Museum of Modern Art* (2006); A. H. Barr Jr., I. Sandler, and E. Newman (eds.), *Defining Modern Art: Selected Writings by Alfred H. Barr Jr.* (1986); M. Scolari Barr, "Our Campaigns": *Alfred H. Barr, Jr., and the Museum of Modern Art: A Biographical Chronicle of the Years 1930–1944* (1987); and R. Roob, "Alfred H. Barr Jr.: A Chronicle of the Years 1902–1929," in *The New Criterion* (special issue, 1987); J. Elderfield (ed.), *The Museum of Modern Art at Mid-Century: Continuity and Change* (1995); J. S. Gordon Kantor, *Alfred H. Barr Jr. and the Intellectual Origins of the Museum of Modern Art* (2002); D. A. Hanks (ed.), *Partners in Design: Alfred H. Barr Jr. and Philip Johnson* (2015). This last publication contains two essays, D. Albrecht's "The High Bohemia of 1930's Manhattan" and B. Bergdoll's "Modern Architecture: International Exhibition," that I used in a direct and indirect manner each time I spoke of MoMA, as also N. F. Weber's *Patron Saints: Five Rebels Who Opened America to a New Art, 1928–1943* (1992) with reference to the environment in which those who promoted the creation of the museum developed. The literature dedicated to MoMA exhibitions in the field of architecture is not as broad as might be expected. Beyond the essay by Bergdoll just noted are J. Elderfield (ed.), *Philip Johnson and the Museum of Modern Art* (1998); T. Riley, *The International Style: Exhibition 15 and the Museum of Modern Art* (1992); and H. Matthew's essay "The Promotion of Modern Architecture by the Museum of Modern

Art in the 1930s," *Journal of Design History*, no. 1 (1994). And critical resources that cannot be left out are: the MoMA catalogues *Modern Architecture: International Exhibition* (1932), *Bauhaus 1919–1928* (1938), and *A New House by Frank Lloyd Wright on Bear Run, Pennsylvania* (1938); the exhibitions *Le Corbusier* (1935), *Frank Lloyd Wright American Architect* (1940), *Mies van der Rohe* (1947, accompanied by the eponymous, famous catalogue by Philip Johnson), and the book by H.-R. Hitchcock and Johnson, *The International Style: Architecture Since 1922* (1932). On Abby Rockefeller, I consulted B. Kert's *Abby Aldrich Rockefeller: The Woman in the Family* (1993).

Regarding the figures who receive the most insistent attention in this book, information about Solomon R. Guggenheim and his family was drawn from M. Lomask's *Seed Money: The Guggenheim Story* (1964), S. Birmingham's *"Our Crowd": The Great Jewish Families of New York* (1967), and J. H. Davis's *The Guggenheims, 1848–1988: An American Epic* (1988).

J. Lukach carried out the most meticulous research on the figure of Baroness von Ehrenwiesen, Hilla Rebay; her study, *Hilla Rebay: In Search of the Spirit in Art* (1983), is exhaustive and well researched. The information it provides derives from Rebay's copious correspondence (letters sent by the baroness to Rudolf Bauer, and those she received from Kandinsky, which I cited, are transcribed in this book). To get to know Rebay, beyond the biography by Lukach I consulted R. Scarlett's *The Baroness, the Mogul, and the Forgotten History of the First Guggenheim Museum as Told by One Who Was There* (2003), and S. Faltin's *Die Baroness und das Guggenheim* (2005). *Art of Tomorrow: Hilla Rebay and Solomon R. Guggenheim* (2005) was the catalogue published on the occasion of the exhibition of the same name held at the Guggenheim Museum. It includes essays by V. Endicott Barnett, J.-A. Birnie Darzker, R. Rosenblum, K. Vail, and R. von Rebay that are useful in various ways for understanding the figures of Rebay and Guggenheim and for bringing into focus the events at the origin of the creation of the Guggenheim Museum. Similarly fruitful reading is the volume edited by K. Vail and published on the fiftieth anniversary of the museum's inauguration, *The Museum of Non-Objective Painting: Hilla Rebay and the Origins of the Solomon Guggenheim Museum* (2009), which includes essays by Vail, T. Bashkoff, J. G. Hanhardt, and D. Quaintance.

Among Rebay's own writings, in addition to the transcript of the interview she gave to B. Hooten, now in the

Archives of American Art (Smithsonian Institution, Washington, D.C.), I consulted "The Definition of Non-Objective Painting," in *Solomon R. Guggenheim Collection of Non-Objective Paintings* (1936); "The Beauty of Non-Objectivity," in *Second Enlarged Catalogue of the Solomon R. Guggenheim Collection of Non-Objective Paintings* (1937); and *Art of Tomorrow: Solomon R. Guggenheim Collection of Non-Objective Paintings* (1939). Lastly, I was able to reconstruct the evolution of the museum's collection of artworks thanks to the two volumes by A. Z. Rudenstine, *The Guggenheim Museum Collections: Paintings, 1880–1945* (1976).

Concerning Rudolf Bauer and his work, in addition to what Rebay wrote in various texts, I drew information from two catalogues: *Rudolf Bauer: Centennial Exhibition* (1989), with the essay by S. Neuburger, "From 'Sturm' to 'Geistreich': Rudolf Bauer in Berlin," and that of S. Lowy, "Rudolf Bauer: A Non-Objective Point of View," in *Rudolf Bauer* (2007). The essays contained in J. Gross, *The Société Anonyme: Modernism for America* (2006), helped me understand the role of the Société Anonyme Inc., founded by Marcel Duchamp, Man Ray, and Katherine S. Dreier, in the diffusion of knowledge of avant-garde art in the United States, and thus, also, in making Bauer a well-known figure among New York collectors.

The theme of "non-objective" art obliges us to continually return to Kandinsky's texts, which I consulted in the versions that can be found in the volumes edited by P. Sers, *Wassily Kandinsky: Tutti gli scritti* (1973 and 1974). While reading Kandinsky's writings, I constantly referred to the essay by A. Kojève, "Les Peintures concrètes de Kandinsky" (1936), and the correspondence published in A. Schönberg, *Wassily Kandinsky: Briefe, Bilder und Dokumente einer außergewöhnlichen Begegnung* (1980), and Schönberg–Busoni, *Schönberg–Kandinsky: Correspondances, textes* (1995). Various exhibitions, accompanied by their catalogues, held in Vienna, Paris, and New York have dealt with the relations between Kandinsky and Schönberg; the last I had the chance to visit, *Arnold Schönberg: Peindre l'âme*, at the Musée d'art et d'histoire du Judaïsme in Paris in 2016, was accompanied by a rather well-constructed catalogue, with excellent illustrations.

Among Rebay's many associates, I devoted particular attention to Frederick Kiesler. Reading some of his numerous articles and brief essays published between 1923 and 1945, on the design of theatrical sets and museums, I found to be as valuable as the article noted above, "Notes on the Spiral Theme in Recent Architecture." A good source of information, including further bibliography and interesting essays devoted to Kiesler, can be found in M. Bottero, *Frederick Kiesler: Arte, architettura, ambiente* (1996), and in the catalogues *Frederick Kiesler Architekt, 1890–1965* (1975), *Friedrick Kiesler* (ed. L. Phillips, 1989), and *Frederick Kiesler: Artiste-architecte* (1996). In studying the figure of Kiesler and his relations with Rebay, it was inevitable that I would come to deal with his links with Peggy Guggenheim. In this, I relied on the catalogue edited by S. Davidson and P. Rylands, *Peggy Guggenheim and Frederick Kiesler: The Story of Art of This Century* (2004). Published on the occasion of the exhibition *Peggy and Kiesler: The Collector and the Visionary* held at the Peggy Guggenheim Collection in Venice, this volume contains essays, in addition to those by the curators, by D. Bogner, F. V. O'Connor, D. Quaintance, V. V. Sanzogni, and J. Sharp, as well as a helpful chronology. Another instructive text is the book by Peggy Guggenheim herself, *Out of This Century: Confessions of an Art Addict* (1979).

There are few publications dedicated to James Johnson Sweeney, and information on him comes from the thesis by T. R. Beauchamp, "James Johnson Sweeney and the Museum of Fine Arts, Houston" (University of Texas at Austin, 1983). What Sweeney wrote following the opening of the Guggenheim Museum, in the article "Chambered Nautilus on Fifth Avenue," appeared in the January 1960 issue of *Museum News*; the same number includes further authoritative contributions, among which those by Mumford, P. Blake, and P. Johnson deserve our attention, as well as his introduction to the book edited by P. Nierendorf, *Paul Klee: Paintings, Watercolors, 1913–1939* (1941), and the book he wrote with J. L. Sert, *Antoni Gaudí* (1960), which is useful in understanding his architectural interests.

Robert Moses, who appears several times in this book, and sometimes as a key figure in the events, has been the object of a sizable amount of literature, which I consulted, favoring the books: R. Moses, *Public Works: A Dangerous Trade* (1970), in which a few pages are devoted to the relations between the author and Wright; R. A. Caro, *The Power Broker: Robert Moses and the Fall of New York* (1974, a tome of over a thousand pages that earned its author a Pulitzer Prize); and the excellent volume of essays by various authors edited by H. Ballon and K. T. Jackson, *Robert Moses and the Modern City: The Transformation of New York* (2007).

In forming the hypotheses I put forward in this book, other texts dedicated to subjects that are not necessarily germane to that of the book contributed to developing the interpretive instruments I used in setting a course for these pages. *The Conscience of the Eye: The Design and Social Life of Cities* (1992) by R. Sennett is recommended for its acute analyses of the mechanisms of urban development in New York City. To interpret the meaning and conception of the spatial layout of the Guggenheim, the transcripts of the lectures given by Pavel Florenskij at VkHUTEMAS in 1923–24 were invaluable; they are translated into English in the volume *Beyond Vision: Essays on the Perception of Art* (2002). In dealing with the meaning of the museum's domed space and speaking of ornament in relation to its configuration, I relied on what A. K. Coomaraswamy wrote in his fundamental essays "Ornament" and "The Symbolism of the Dome," now in *Coomaraswamy: Selected Papers* (ed. R. E. Lipsey, vol. 1, 1977). Taking the essays of Coomaraswamy as a starting point, and having reconsidered what Levine wrote in note 9 of his chapter on the Guggenheim in his book *The Architecture of Frank Lloyd Wright*, I came, tangentially, to speak of the "reversibility" of the edifice Wright built, with a strong memory in my mind of the pages titled "La yaksi y la Virgen," in O. Paz's *Conjunciones y disyunciones* (1991). Through this path, however, the idea of defining the Guggenheim as an iconoclastic building grew clear. This is not the place to dwell on the question of iconoclasm, which runs through our history from the pre-Socratics onward, and it would be presumptuous to draw any bibliographic reference from such an immense body of literature. However, I think I must mention two sources: on the modern cult of museums, I had before me the pages of *In Praise of Folly* (1511), in which Erasmus writes of "superstitions" (also in relationship to his peculiar attitude toward iconoclasm this great book is enlightening). While I pondered how to explain the Guggenheim's aniconism, I was pleased to reread D. Freedberg's wonderful book, *The Power of Images: Studies in the History and Theory of Response* (1989).

What is the meaning that museums have taken on in our time, and to what extent can what these institutions represent help in understanding a work so exceptional as that which Wright built for Solomon Guggenheim in New York? While this may not have been the question that I asked myself when I began to write this book, I know for certain that it accompanied me constantly, and continues to do so. The terms in which it originally appeared to me can be summed up in this passage from Ernst Jünger: "The world we live in displays on the one hand positive similarities to a workshop and on the other to a museum. The distinction between these two landscapes, from the point of view of the demands they imply, is that no one is forced to see in a workshop more than simply a workshop whereas over the museum landscape there reigns a grotesquely proportioned spirit of edification. We have risen to a level of historical fetishism that stands in a direct relation to our deficiency in productive energy. Therefore the dismal thought occurs that some sort of secret correspondence causes the pace of our accumulation and preservation of so-called cultural goods to be matched only by the grandiose scale on which we simultaneously create instruments of destruction." This passage can be found in *Der Arbeiter* (1932); it explains the significance of the inscriptions by Paul Valéry on the façade of the Palais de Chaillot in Paris: "Ami, n'entre pas sans désir" (Friend, enter not without desire) and introduces one of the great essays Jünger dedicated to the phenomenology of the Modern, *An der Zeitmauer* (1959), to which I often turn.

The way in which I dealt with the role assumed by the museum in the contemporary world owes much to M. Fumaroli's *L'État culturel* (1991) and J. Clair's *Considérations sur l'état des beaux arts: Critique de la modernité* (1983). Lastly, I will make a few, succinct notes on what I have read while considering the theme of collectors and patrons, an association that is at the origin of many American museums. There is a vast field of literature on this subject, from which I selected *A Market for Merchant Princes* (2015), edited by I. Reist, and W. Craven's *Stanford White: Decorator in Opulence and Dealer in Antiquities* (2005). As usual, when I study subjects or matters relating to the United States of America, and this was no exception, Jean Baudrillard's *America* (1986) was always at my side.

Acknowledgments

While preparing this book I discussed with a few friends as I was writing; the most patient ones read my first, handwritten manuscript; each of these friends, but Nicholas Adams and Tomaso Trombetti especially, with the book before them, will be able to judge the debts I have amassed. I owe a particular debt to Katherine Boller, her colleagues at Yale University Press, and Sarah Melker, who patiently translated my words.

I first visited the Solomon R. Guggenheim Museum in 1971. From that moment the Guggenheim became a destination I cannot turn down each time I find myself in New York. I decided, however, to write this book after having traveled to New York with Bastiana, and returned there with her when well over thirty years had passed since that first visit. For this reason, too, but not only, I dedicate this book to her.

Venezia, October 2016

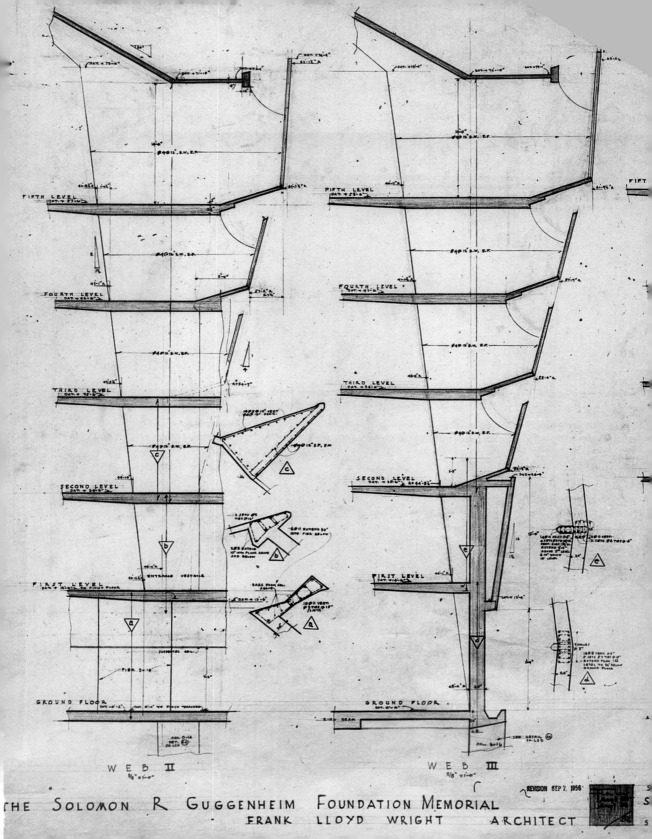

WEB II

WEB III

REVISION SEP 7, 1956

THE SOLOMON R GUGGENHEIM FOUNDATION MEMORIAL

FRANK LLOYD WRIGHT ARCHITECT

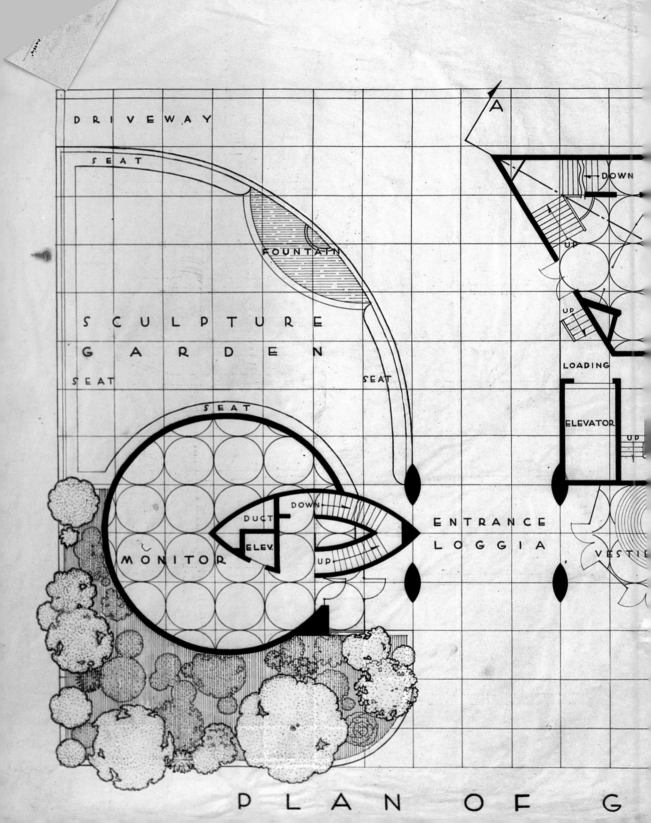

DRIVEWAY

SEAT

FOUNTAIN

SCULPTURE
GARDEN

SEAT

SEAT

SEAT

A

DOWN

UP

UP

LOADING

ELEVATOR

UP

DOWN

DUCT

ELEV.

UP

MONITOR

ENTRANCE
LOGGIA

VESTI

P L A N   O F   G